Soul Quest of the Dancing Butterfly

Soul Quest of the Dancing Butterfly:

Twelve Steps to Spiritual Wholeness

By:

Hugh Leroy Thompson

ISBN: 979-8-89034-690-2

Library of Congress Control Number: 2024906694

Scripture taken from THE MESSAGE (MSG), by Eugene H. Peterson, copyright © 1993, 1994, 1995, 1996, 2000, 2001, 2002 has provisional permission "providing the verses quoted do not amount to a complete book of the Bible and do not account for twenty-five percent or more of the total text of the work in which they are quoted."

The English Standard Version (ESV) text may be quoted (in written or print form) up to and inclusive of five hundred (500) verses without express written permission of the publisher, providing that the verses quoted do not amount to more than one-half of any one book of the Bible nor do the verses quoted account for 25 percent or more of the total text of the work in which they are quoted.

The New International Version (NIV) text may be quoted in any form (written, visual, electronic, or audio), up to and inclusive of five hundred (500) verses without the express written permission of the publisher, providing the verses quoted do not amount to a complete book of the Bible, nor do verses quoted account for 25 percent or more of the total text of the work in which they are quoted.

Although I am an ordained minister and professional counselor, reading this book does not create a professional relationship between us. This book should not be used as a substitute for the advice of a competent spiritual guide (clergy), mental health counselor, or medical practitioner authorized or licensed to practice in their professional jurisdiction.

Dedication

To D. Sharon Thompson, my life partner, best friend, and soulmate. She was a constant source of affirmation and encouragement and a loving critic. I cherish our wonderful memories and the many sacred moments of the journey we shared.

Table of Contents

Introduction

Do you feel spiritually empty, and does your soul seem malnourished? Is there a "blue cloud" hovering overhead? We all have support systems, but for some, there are extended periods of anguish or, at best, depression. Life seems complicated. You fail to recognize the paradoxes of life and death, joy and sorrow, hope and despair. However, each happening allows you to discover the natural rhythms of your existence that are beating together in syncopation.

There's been a significant increase in those seeking alternatives to traditional religion or institutionalized churches emphasizing doctrines or restricted interpretations of sacred writings, including biblical traditions. Many conventional Christian churches are converting their worship practices to appeal to those who want more contemporary experiences. Worship has become so "electrified" and "videoed" to attract the newer generation's language and values. Technology is more important than theology to many today. There's a longing for spirituality, yet many do not know what that means.

Most of us long to make sense of our personal lives and to find purpose with meaning. Life's a composition of heartbreak and happiness, sickness and healing, loneliness and fellowship, brokenness and wholeness. These experiences aren't opposites of each other; they flow together and can transform your life's activities. This book will offer the possibilities of newness for your spirit and refreshment for your soul. You will discover how God's Spirit energizes and empowers your mind–body–soul. I've chosen the image of the dancing butterfly for a specific reason.

The butterfly is a beautiful metaphor revealing the rhythms of the evolving soul in each of us. The butterfly symbolizes the soul in many religious and spiritual traditions, including Christianity. It's about the metamorphosis or change that occurs throughout different life cycles. It's primarily associated with renewal and rebirth. You'll read about how this can happen in your life.

There are twelve steps you can practice, which will guide you into spiritual wholeness. These aren't the Twelve Steps of Alcoholics Anonymous, but one can find a parallel. The Twelve Steps to Spiritual Wholeness offer no effort or intent as an alternative for those recovering from an addiction.

First, complete your twelve-step program, practicing abstinence, sobriety, and recovery. The steps offered in this book can guide you on a journey of hope, regardless of your spiritual or religious beliefs. I developed them more than forty years ago and distributed them to the organizations and churches where I preached or trained. Being encouraged to expand the meaning of each one gave me the desire to create the book. Hopefully, it will be of value to you.

You wouldn't be reading this if you had little interest in your spirituality. While there will be biblical references, don't be concerned if your religious or nonreligious tradition differs from the Christian perspective. The term "spiritual wholeness" is inclusive, and the *Soul Quest of the Dancing Butterfly; Twelve Steps to Spiritual Wholeness* is all-encompassing. The word *God* is universally acknowledged as the Creator or Spiritual Force who is an abiding presence in all of life. It's the premise on which these steps are written. Your spiritual quest shouldn't be limited by language. The "healthy soul" is open and vulnerable to God's Spirit wherever the journey goes.

Second, understand how your soul can become sick, the contributing factors, and how wellness can be achieved. Some of your spiritual sabotaging will be exposed, and what can you do to break these habits?

A word of caution if you choose to embrace these twelve steps. Each step takes time to internalize; you'll want to read and apply the steps daily. All twelve-step programs, including these, emphasize practicing them in "all of your *daily* affairs." Each step will challenge your mind, heart, and soul, so prepare for deep reflection and meditation.

Although my background includes being a member of the clergy in the Christian tradition, I've discovered spiritual insight and guidance from Hinduism, Buddhism, the Baha'i teachings, and historical Judaism. I've found meaning in spirituality, with a deep appreciation of inclusivity and general faith beliefs beyond the norm. My spiritual quest gives me a broader scope than traditional

Christianity and institutional religion. You'll find various references and thoughts identified as you read. I'll always be a seeker and wish the same for you. I admit that these religions' variations of beliefs and teachings aren't the same. Their differences are important, yet they have some common interpretations of spirituality, spiritual wholeness, and loving care of others worthy of acknowledgment.

Each step of the *Twelve Steps to Spiritual Wholeness* is designed to guide you in realizing spiritual maturity as you practice these steps. I acknowledge the need for caution whenever you're making life-altering decisions. This process will naturally impact your mind and body. Having a personal physician who can be available to monitor your health is basic. It may be wise to have a physical before you start this quest.

Are there only twelve steps? No, there are other authors and therapists with alternative approaches. Will these steps assure me that I can become spiritually whole? They will help you grow with no guarantees of complete success. You may need to acquire what's called "ambiguity tolerance," which is the ability to tolerate the range of options to be considered. It's admitting that some "truth" or "belief" falls in a gray or debatable area.

My years of experience, training, and counseling practice have contributed to this book. The educational and clinical training prepared me to help and care for those searching to resolve their pain and suffering, holding them captive to unhealthy and destructive habits. I'm always in prayerful thought and sincere concern for the well-being of any reader. I've provided ministry and counseling to countless individuals and families struggling to survive their anguish and brokenness. I'm blessed that God has given me the heart and gifts to be a healing mentor. I'm filled with humility and gratitude to those who trusted my care and love for them.

One final suggestion is to cultivate the discipline of keeping a personal spiritual journal. I would encourage you to complete the "Spiritual Inventory" in chapter eight. But complete the seven chapters before attempting the inventory. During your quest, you may experience several awakenings that will free your soul to join the butterfly's dance and discover more about who and what you are. Recycling through each step for reinforcement and clarity is natural before taking the next step. Remaining open to new adventures is a mixture of excitement and uncertainty!

One

QUEST OF YOUR SOUL

Our Soul is the sacred essence within us; our deepest purpose,
unique meaning, and guiding force behind our individual lives.
—Mateo Sol (LonerWolf.com)

I've always been fascinated by butterflies. In high school, I studied them and made a collection, organizing each butterfly species in glass-framed cases. My mother thought it was cruel to pin them to a display board and place them in "boxes." I explained that their life span averaged about a month, but this didn't ease her mind.

Through the years, I've planted flowers to attract these fascinating insects and still watch the beauty and elegance of all the varieties as they dance between the flowers, searching for nectar. My grandchildren delight in the arrival of the monarch butterflies and sit like stone statues, anticipating one landing on their head or finger. The child in all of us never tires of gazing at one of nature's magical creatures.

The butterfly, for centuries, has been linked to the myth of the psyche. Aristotle gave the butterfly the name *psyche*, the Greek word for *soul*. The myth signifies the human search for what is authentic, meaningful, and essential. Why the image of the butterfly? Because it's free from death, the soul's body can fly freely, soaring away, and leaving the chains of the chrysalis. Once freed, it dances the celebration of new life and seeks the nectar of the flowers.

The dancing butterfly illustrates the splendor of the unfolding of one's soul in the quest for spiritual wholeness. Many Native American legends perform a butterfly dance to petition for the healing of all living things. They pay tribute to the annual cycle of seasonal renewal.

Mystery writer Laurie Buchanan shares a beautiful version of this folklore:

There's an American Indian legend—some say it's Cherokee, others Shoshone—that a butterfly woman lost her mate in a war. Grief-stricken, she took off her wings, wrapped herself in a cocoon, and went on a long journey. She walked carefully, stepping stones as she went, and saw a very beautiful stone. Her sadness ended at the sight of this stone. Throwing off the cocoon, she put on her wings again and danced joyfully. To this day, her tribe dances the Butterfly Dance to greet new seasons, new life, and new beginnings. In the world of totems, the butterfly is a symbol of change, joy, love, and metamorphosis. Not overnight, but the butterfly morphs in a series of four stages:
Egg—fertilization, giving birth.
Larva—strengthening the foundation.
Chrysalis—cocooning for reorganization
Butterfly—emerging in lightness and joy.[1]

I appreciate how she identifies the four stages of growth. It's the primary focus of your soul quest and the significance of the twelve steps. Commit yourself to experiencing and adopting the transformation of each stage.

Spirituality and Wholeness

Outside your daily awareness, at a deeper level, your soul longs for inner peace and outer balance. The busyness of your life prevents any resolution to this constant toil. Father Ronald Rolheiser, a Catholic priest and theologian, agrees: "It is no easy task to walk this earth and find peace. Inside of us, it would seem, something is at odds with the very rhythm of things, and we are forever restless, dissatisfied, frustrated, and aching."[2]

Today, much of what we call spirituality is the outgrowth of a depletion complex. This complex is born from weakness and inadequacy as we clamor for a power that lifts us from our depression, doldrums, addictions, or other debilitating situations. We tend to believe that God is there as our depletion allowance. Such an idea is rooted in an obsessive pursuit of a God who will help us overcome our ineptitude or lack of self-confidence.

Although it's true that God doesn't expect you to "lift yourself by your bootstraps," neither can you frantically run to God, hoping your trials and tribulations will be taken away. It's a naive, even saccharine, image of God. God doesn't complete you. God created you whole. Your genesis is birthed out of God's power and given to you as a part of your created humanity and evolving divinity. God's power complements your human power.

Our integrity and responsibility as dwellers on this earth are to be in a cocreative copartnership with God. God didn't create us to be dependent children who continuously run home when we seem unable to handle our affairs. You're in an interdependent covenant with God to be accountable for your decisions and responsible for the consequences of those choices. Today is the best opportunity to walk with God rather than have God carry you through all that is before you. Do you trust this much?

Spiritual versus Religious Perceptions

You're on a holy mission, not a religious destination. Your soul isn't searching for heavenly salvation; you seek to know a heaven on earth that brings fullness to your whole being. The problem with the alcoholic or addict is the tendency to use God, religious beliefs, or a deviation of spirituality to escape any emotional or physical pain.

Today, one of my biggest concerns is witnessing the growth of religiously overdeveloped people who are spiritually atrophying or dying. Ralph Waldo Emerson felt the same in his day: "Once we had wooden chalices and golden priests; now we have golden chalices and wooden priests."[3] He's acknowledging his concern about too many clergy members having this relationship with the institutional church. We're forever building the church and killing the spirit. The church dies when form, creed, and doctrine triumph over the mind.

When the building or structures grow, and we lose our (*en-theos*) enthusiasm, God's Spirit is diminished. I don't believe you're looking for a "religious experience" as much as seeking "spiritual nourishment" or a soulful experience. Today, the overabundance of religion and too little spirituality appears.

Religious power and spiritual truth aren't synonymous. Our religion, faith, beliefs, and operating values are widely separated. Just because the Gallup poll reports 94 percent of Americans believe in God doesn't in any way give credence to the belief that we're a spiritually mature nation; in fact, we're far from it. Sam Keen, in his tribute *Hymns to an Unknown God*, upholds this notion: "I can't go back to traditional religion. Neither can I live within the smog-bound horizon of the secular-progressive faith. So, I search for a way to unite the demands of the head and the heart."[4]

Erich Fromm, a prominent German psychologist, developed two basic personality types identified as the necrophile—a destructive, perverted personality attracted to death—and the biophile—an optimistic personality attracted to life. Biophiles love life and all that is alive. They wish to grow and explore—open to every expanding truth continually. Necrophiles are frightened of novelty and uncertainty. They are anxious to get to heaven.[5] We're to be spiritually alive, not anxiously waiting for our arrival at the gates of glory. We're on a journey filled with excitement and possibilities, but this excursion has no guaranteed future; we can only depend on the Divine Spirit to lead us into a new day with all the hesitations we face.

The religious among us want to have absolutes and expect to know God's mapped-out plan, while the spiritual ones are satisfied with the adventure to explore, be known by God, and walk an uncharted path. The religious seek to ascend, living on higher ground, rising above it all. Spiritual life descends to the depths of human existence and is present in suffering and healing. Many have adopted strange and dangerous metaphors for the church. Some consider it like a business. Church members are the financial "bottom line" impacting its mission and outreach. Churches look to the latest marketing strategies to attain growth and mimic religious rock music concerts. Another popular view is treating the church as a country club. A few of the members attend worship to be visible to other socialites. They contribute financially so the church will offer a variety of "social" ministries and truly create opportunities for "fellowship."

The most disturbing concept of the church is the court of moral justice (judgment). The teachings and doctrines emphasize the "sins" of the people. It defines and enforces the mindset and religious beliefs that follow the strict adherence to the "absolute" truths of the Bible (no variations). There's no tolerance for deviation from biblical "certainty." No wonder cynics and pessimists want to persuade you that the only signs are despair and a future winding down, moving toward a dead end. However, there's Good News with a better ending. Snoopy, the wise dog from the *Peanuts* comic strip, won't let the discouraging words of Lucy, the cynic, stop him from dancing. Lucy hollers words of despair: "Floods! Famine! Doom! Fire! Hell!" Snoopy continues to dance, undaunted by her defeatism. Lucy resigns her effort and starts dancing with Snoopy: "Well, if you can't defeat 'em, join 'em!"

Expectantly, your spiritual quest seeks transformation and continual growth, a longing for God to inspire your spirit and soul to dance to life's rhythms of joy and fulfillment. Since you can only see the world through your eyes, make it however you hope. But you need to be decisive. You can't get closer to God by living carelessly or incidentally. Your soul quest is intentional and intense. There's nothing casual about this process. It involves being thoughtful and focused. Celebrate with the Psalmist: "You have turned for me my mourning into dancing; you have loosed my sackcloth and clothed me with gladness" (Ps. 30:11, ESV).

Two

THE SICKNESS OF YOUR SOUL

We suffer from a spiritual autoimmune disease. Lacking antibodies
of faith to keep us from despair, we attack ourselves.
—Sandor McNab, in Sam Keen's *In the Absence of God*

Does your soul dance to the joyful rhythms of life? Can you celebrate the beauty surrounding your world, or has the music gone mute, the beat of the drum having lost its cadence? Most likely, you fluctuate between the extremes. Before your journey to spiritual wholeness, look back and see how you got where you are. How does your soul become ill in the first place? Soul sickness has no significance without first attempting to understand what is meant by the human soul. You may even experience the absence of God and find little comfort in healing your soul. The absence of the soul creates a life devoid of the sacred and mysterious; an agonizing existence is "hell on earth."

It's a genuine question: "What precisely is the soul?" Every philosopher, psychologist, theologian, poet, and great author ad nauseam has studied and written about this inquiry. Volumes of literature have devoted endless themes regarding the human soul. Dr. Albert Schweitzer believed,

No one can give a definition of the soul. But we know what it feels like. The soul is the sense of something higher than ourselves, something that stirs in us thoughts, hopes, and aspirations that go out to the world of goodness, truth, and beauty. The soul is a burning desire to breathe in this world of light and never to lose it—to remain children of light.[6]

There's no verifiable evidence we have souls. Any definition is but a false effort to mask the unidentifiable. Yet experience teaches us there is a realm of reality beyond our physicality and mentality. Ancient religious traditions believed the soul energizes the body. Aristotle opposed the notion that the soul could exist apart from the body. More traditional Jewish thought adopts this same principle. Many biblical scholars claim the symbiosis of soul and spirit is punctuated in the Old Testament, arguing that the spirit synergizes the human body, mind, and soul. Suffice it to say, let's leave this dispute to the world of academia and settle on a more practical note.

This passionate quest has ventured down lonely roads, deep caverns, dark valleys, and arid deserts. I didn't discover my soul; my soul continually brought me disturbance, agony, annoyance, and restlessness, where I could no longer hide. The soul is the essence of your whole being; without the soul, you *are* "dry bones"—you are a vacuum as vast as the black hole of space. The soul is your passion for life, giving ultimate meaning. The true self hints at what is called the soul. It isn't an object but a value or a way of experiencing your life.

How's the soul distinguished from the spirit? Greek has words for the soul *(psuchē)* and spirit *(pneuma)*. The spirit is the "divine spark" in us. It awakens the transcendent dimension of life; it communicates God's eternal truths; it recognizes the life principle bestowed by God.

The Hebrew word for "soul" is *nephesh,* and "spirit" is *ruach,* meaning "breath"; God breathed life into human creation. In most languages, including English, these words have various meanings and usages. Soul and spirit are associated with human personas and are more like verbs than nouns, suggesting "animation," vibrancy, and energy, continually renewing life. Your soul is inherent, internal, and intrinsic; it's your inner self. Your spirit is transcendent, mystical, and unlimited; it's your higher self.

What about your body and mind? How do these aspects of your humanness involve the soul's quest for spiritual wholeness? The Greek word *nous* denotes "*mind.*" Your mind is the seat of reflective consciousness, including perception, understanding, judging, and determining. Importantly, your mind has the function of moral thinking and ethical impulse.

Your mind also is the center of imagination and intellect. The Baha'i faith has a beautiful way of illuminating this idea: "But the mind is the power of the human spirit. Spirit is the lamp; the mind is the light that shines from the lamp. Spirit is the tree, and the mind is the fruit. Mind is the perfection of the spirit and is its essential quality, as the sun's rays are the essential necessity of the sun."[7]

Body is your physical presence in the world. The Greek name for body is *soma*. Basically, this term signifies "the instrument of life." The body is best known to modern science and medicine and comprises the skeletal framework, muscles, tissues, organs, blood, and the five senses: sight, smell, taste, touch, and hearing. Your body is earthbound; death brings finality to your physical being. Your body is the means for physical connection to another person. Physical attraction (seven senses) is one dynamic in building relationships, but it isn't adequate for continuing a relationship; love and the fulfillment of life happen through the healthy communication between your body and mind, the unity of one through the Holy One.

I've used a broad brush to paint the landscape of your identity. Who you are is more complex and comprehensive than your body, mind, soul, and spirit. The interaction and explanation of your history on this planet are determined by the commitment to live your whole life with spiritual wholeness.

Soul Sickness

Psychosomatic (*psyche*, mind; *soma*, body) illness was once considered only psychological, not physical. When a physician can't diagnose physical symptoms, he may refer to a medical specialist performing "psycho-physiology." This kind of physician medically assesses the interaction of mind and body on the nervous system. They tell us that all sickness is real.

Sickness confronts you with the reality that your body never deceives. You may tell others and even yourself that everything is fine, but intrinsically, your body knows better. You've been ignoring your body's messages; the body cries, "No!" *No* to the overextension of time; *no* to poor eating habits; *no* to the lack of exercise; and *no* to the neglect of emotional, mental, physical, and spiritual care. The failure to be a good steward of your whole self has its own set of consequences. Your soul becomes silent, your energy wanes, and your mind denies the truth, overriding all verbal protests. You're caught in the pathology of a demoralizing and spiritually agonizing illness. What happens when you make the wrong choices or resign yourself to doing nothing?

Spiritual Pathology

In my early years of ministry and addiction counseling, I sought to understand a theoretical basis for the pathology of "soul sickness." I was trained in the psychosomatic nature of the disease. However, my curiosity and need to know about the spiritual pathology was compelling. I studied and researched the subject until I discovered the foundation to explain the symptoms, attitudes, phobias, and voids occurring in those affected by any problems related to spiritual health. It's inclusive and doesn't apply only to addictions. Indeed, there are additional effects and symptoms besides the ones mentioned here.

There are five overarching symptoms with subsequent attitudes, phobias, and voids. The symptoms of soul sickness are progressive, and you may not have all the indicators. The longer, more acute, and chronic the pathology, the more serious. Hopefully, you'll find options for change and avenues for discovering spiritual health.

Ontic Anxiety

Symptoms: The Greek root word for *ontic* is *ontos,* indicating "being" or "becoming." It's a basic fear of "living" rather than dying. A nonrational dependence on rigid beliefs, values, and dogmas evidences this fear of being and becoming. An example would be the individual who defends his family from outsiders yet physically abuses them. He may believe that the family must stay together, no matter what happens, and fears anyone or anything that would interfere.

Attitudes: "This is the way things are! Just accept it! I can't change who I am!" The more out of control your life becomes, the more the need for security and certainty escalates. You become more rigid and unbending about making decisions or going places. The anxiety of change and unpredictability increases dysfunctional coping and defense skills, such as drinking and medicating the anxiety, compulsively spending, and gambling to fill your emptiness. You may even engage in inappropriate sexual activity for immediate gratification. You begin feeling like life is spiraling downward, the more you indulge in this behavior.

Phobias: You fear having no choices and options or making the wrong decision. The distinction between mental and ontic anxiety is the locus of your fear. Cognitive anxiety is typically a reaction to an unreal or imagined danger. It usually indicates that the body–mind is overwhelmed concerning one's subjective ability to deal with a particular situation. It's sometimes referred to as "performance fear." Fritz Perls, noted psychiatrist and developer of Gestalt therapy, called it "stage fright."

Ontic anxiety, on the other hand, points to the soulful distress of resisting being "born." It's the naive persistence of a Popeye mentality, declaring, "I am who I am." It's the unwillingness to acknowledge that "I am always becoming." It's the disturbing restlessness of answering the question, "Is there life after birth?" The alcoholic or drug addict only knows a "living death." As one teenager said, when asked what his epitaph would be, he stated, "Died at sixteen and buried at thirty." This is called "a living death."

Voids: Your foundation of faith has crumbled; ontic anxiety is the antithesis of faith. Faith allows you to live with life's absurdities and uncertainties. Faith doesn't guarantee the inner strength to walk the path to spiritual wholeness and accept "one day at a time." Faith isn't the opposite of doubt; it's the need for certainty. Radical fundamentalism claims God is absolute and demands strict adherence to the infallibility of the Bible. You might want to read *The Gospel According to Thomas*.[8] It could alter your need for guarantees.

Anxiety undermines your faith, and your mind won't open a new perspective on life. You have no, or insufficient, faith to venture into the unknown without a map for the journey. Many are disillusioned with the beliefs and values of secular life. Countless more are indifferent to established religion. Its conventional witness to spiritual meaning is tepid, offering little to life's meaning, values, or sense of the sacred presence of a Divine Being. There seems to be a vague spiritual urge to discover authentic "soul" nourishment but remain "spiritually empty."

Self-Exaggeration

Symptoms: "Ego-theism" or "self-deification." It's revealed by your embellished self-concept with a deluded sense of self-sufficiency and reflected in the "I-It" versus "I-Thou" approach to interpersonal relationships. The "god-like" character begins to envelop your very being. Even when your world is disintegrating, you always insist that everything is OK and that you "don't need anything from anybody."

Your daily interactions successfully pump the ego, and you regard yourself as the center of the world. You conceive persons as self-extensions of *you*. Some current authors argue that ego-theism is the new atheism of the age.

In one of my quiet, reflective moments, I struggled with this paradox and wrote this verse:

My Ego doesn't like a self-audit.
>Yet I know such an inventory is essential in my journey to be whole.
Everywhere I go, my Ego demands to follow.
While I find pleasure in giving.
My Ego pursues the rewards of personal gain.
I long only to be centered in life.
My Ego thrives on being the center of life.
>My Ego hungers for a new car, a new home, a new wardrobe—for the moment.
>But I am satisfied with a warm embrace, a gentle breeze, a stroll through the woods, and this moment.
What is it that my Ego feverishly seeks?
That I seemingly give no care?
Is it fame, wealth, security, or immortality?
My Ego is anxious and seeks the answers.
I am content in living before God with the questions.
My Ego compulsively ventures for lasting certainties.
Yet I find serenity in life's serendipitous events.
This leaves one truly unanswered question,
Am I me or my ego?[9]

I recall a woman telling a friend about her husband, "We have a three-way relationship; he and I are both in love with him." Some people have no awareness of how self-centered they are. They would insist on being described as "self-confident" rather than self-obsessed.

Attitudes: You're mainly concerned with your interests. Do you have little or no empathy for others? Are you insensitive to the feelings of those around you? The more territorial you act, the more your whole being experiences disharmony and alienation. You get angry that others don't understand you; you complain, work bitterly, retaliate, and become oversensitive and easily offended. You wake up to a dark and lonely world each day.

You feel abandoned and misunderstood. You cry out, "Their opinions suck! Curse them anyway!" and "I can handle my life! I don't need anyone!"

Phobias: You have a fear of being controlled or losing control. The notion of "surrender" isn't in your vocabulary. You don't need to micromanage the affairs of others. Perhaps you're a victim of childhood trauma due to emotional and physical abuse. You developed the skills of protecting yourself by building emotional and spiritual barriers. You couldn't afford to surrender to someone else's power over you. You became a survivor at the expense of developing healthy self-esteem and meaningful relationships.

Surrender seems nearly universal in the esoteric spiritual practices of many religions and spiritual traditions. It appears to be a constantly emergent theme when we examine the lives of saints, sages, and mystics across time. However, your soul and spirit are bound by your preoccupation with egocentric actions. Surrender is transcendent and occurs only in the realm of humility.

Voids: Selfishness and exaggerated ego are anathemas to the very nature of God's creation. Ego-theism is absent of humility. James knew this: "God opposes the proud but gives grace to the humble" (James 4:6, ESV).

Humility acknowledges that you don't always have to know or have the answer. It's manifested in your daily interactions by yielding to the needs of others rather than focusing on what you want. It has been said that humility grows in the desert. In your loneliest moments, when you have no friend for support, your soul hungers for a warm embrace. God's Spirit fills your emptiness with humility. It isn't self-negation or self-punishment. You only need to surrender.

Emotional and Social Isolation

Symptoms: Your alienation from life's spiritual center and meaning shows this. You isolate yourself from significant others, God's Spirit, and your authentic self. You feel empty, restless, and alone. It's involuntary and distinct from loneliness, a temporary lack of contact with others.

Emotional isolation suffers when your feelings are in check with others. You don't disclose your emotions; you shut down, sense numbness, and refuse to engage in "serious" conversation except superficially. Consequently, emotional detachment is one source of social isolation. Your insecurity— your fear of being judged, disrespected, or misunderstood—worsens relationships. Others may keep their distance from you, completing the cycle of total isolation.

Attitudes: You sense being out of harmony with life. You argue that others are out of tune and don't appreciate your music. Your theme: "Everyone for themselves! Get before you're gotten!"

You develop a hostile attitude and wage war (conflict) with anyone willing to enter the fray. You think what fools they are; they'll never defeat you: "I am a rock!" You have become a "Hard-Hearted Hannah" or a "Macho Man."

Phobias: Humans are created as social beings and seek to be in a community with others. When you become a "victim" of emotional or social isolation, you fear being known, vulnerable, and unable to receive or give love. The more you refuse to hear "negative" feedback, the more rigid and irrational your opinions become; your perceptions are distorted, and your feelings are amplified. You trust no one, believing kindness toward you isn't genuine, only manipulative. Fear of intimacy is paramount.

Void: You awake one day without love and honest relationships. An open relationship isn't dominated by the ego focused on image-making and self-seeking. Meaningful relationships flow outward with openness, being attentive toward the other person without expectations. God's Sacred Presence fills you with deep love and care. It's the prerequisite for any authentic relationship.

Often, this void is fruitlessly filled by different compulsive behaviors: overeating, substance abuse, overcompensating for lack of self-worth (perfectionism), or indulging in fantasy to avoid reality. You may have *people* in your life, but they're mere *objects* to fill your insatiable emptiness and aloneness. You treat them like possessions; when the candy machine goes empty, "friends" are discarded for a different candy flavor.

Spiritual Apathy

Symptoms: Spiritual apathy has been called "a paralysis of the heart." The author of Ephesians observed this state: "They have become callous and have given themselves up to sensuality, greedy to practice every kind of impurity" (Eph. 4:19, ESV). One of the synonyms for paralysis is *numbness*. When you're numb, there is a loss of feeling; you're out of touch and emotionally and spiritually frozen. The Greek word *pathos* means "without suffering." Therefore, a hard shell has formed around your heart and soul, leaving you constricted and insensitive to your inner needs and those of others.

Attitudes: You have no desire to be engaged in caring for human suffering. Your mantra is, "I don't care! That's not my problem!" You feel physically exhausted and emotionally unresponsive. You've lost excitement or interest in almost everything. You become demoralized, and self-care is neglected. In the extreme, some observers may claim you have a "zombielike" appearance.

Phobias: This symptom exhibits fear of zeal and commitment. One of the emotional truths about life is that when you control one feeling, all your feelings are blocked. You've no access to positive feelings when attempting to avoid negative ones. Your soul is your emotional center. Your mind creates a veil of illusion, thinking feelings of pain and suffering, joy, and bliss are merely thoughts; just change your thinking and feelings. What a distortion of reality.

Depression, loneliness, and despair are natural emotions that you would like to avoid. When you've felt each of these in your darkest hours, and they drain your physical energy and spiritual zeal, you want the agony to cease. You distance yourself from these feelings by building an impenetrable fort. Apathy rescues you from those "enemies" of destruction. But apathy robs you of zest and excitement about life; it keeps you locked away from committing yourself to meaningful, supportive relationships or sustaining a marital one.

Voids: Your indifference and lack of emotional investment result in the absence of passion. You've lost connection with your soul's spark for life. God's Spirit is unable to penetrate the barrier of your spirit. When a child is born, you see joy and passion in his eyes. He's a free spirit; his soul longs for the life before him. The growing-up years can take a toll on an infant's native excitement. The family environment and daily affirmations have everything to do with his development as a healthy child. Along the way, he forms a self-identity, self-worth, self-respect, or the failure of each one. Circumstances, experiences, and other influences can steal his zest for life. Your inner child stores memories and experiences of emotional and physical "scars" that shape your view of life.

Passion is innate, and it provides the creative *drive* to celebrate life and immerse yourself in all possibilities one can imagine. Passion fuels your imagination and the desire to have friends, form lasting relationships, and discover the power of love. When your passion dies, your will to live takes the last breath.

Death Obsession or Fantasy

Symptoms: Most humans search for the meaning and mystery of death. It's in our DNA to be concerned about the finality of life as we know it. Though subconsciously, I'm not equating this symptom with those who want to experiment with near-death experiences, but there could be a connection with "death obsession." There are cases of suicides masked as near-death investigations. In contrast, many trot through life and give no thought to death (denial). They insist that life is for the living and that death will take care of itself.

How does death fit in with soul sickness? If your spiritual life has escalated to this level of deep space, convincing you it's one option for ending the absence of love and your apathetic indifference to all that matters, then you have the "virus." You're trapped in melancholia (tearful sadness and irrational fears) and have no choice. Death permits you to avoid all the previous fears we have reviewed. You won't be required to change, alter your life, or rearrange what's of lasting value. You know you must act with courage, and you doubt your inner strength to act.

It isn't suicidal ideation. You aren't projecting a plan to end your life; you only want the pain to cease. Death appears to tranquilize your agony, not bring down the final curtain; though suicide has a parallel, you search for a different option.

I encourage you to seek professional help if you have suicidal thoughts.

Death fantasy is a retreat into your imagination by reading books and watching movies with themes of death. You identify with the main character and begin internalizing the feelings associated with the role. This fictional world takes on "reality," and you have difficulty differentiating your struggle from the actor's.

Attitudes: You hear a familiar voice: "I long for peace beyond the grave!" This is the kind of death obsession that's debilitating; it surfaces as false hope to your hopelessness. Your myopic perception or fantasy is that death offers your soul peace right now.

Phobias: The ultimate fear is that you have no purpose or "calling" in this life. Death looks more inviting than life. You wrestle not with the certainty of death but the uncertainty of life. You ask, "Is there life after birth?" You grapple with "Who am I?" or "What am I to do?" You're scared you have nothing to contribute to this life.

Voids: You arrive at a destination point with the absence of peace, hope, and meaning. Your mind endlessly races, and you feel your brain will explode. You can't escape the "mindless chatter" keeping you awake at night. Your energy is zapped, and you think you will go crazy, needing to be locked away. You anxiously search for inner peace and serenity to no avail.

Hope may be foreign to everything you know. Hope is a feeling of optimism, a sense that things will improve. Hope is an internal awareness that you can manage suffering and despair if you maintain hopeful expectancy in your heart.

Hopelessness is the sentiment of being alienated from God or your Higher Power. You have limited or no spiritual foundation. Life isn't about happiness. It has to do with fulfillment and meaning. God has a benevolent purpose for you. You might doubt this truth, but your presence in this moment of history proves that you are essential and that a mission must be acted out. Meaning and mission are richer concepts than vocation, career, and profession. The interface is integrated into your purpose. Life's more than doing and being; it includes becoming, planting, sharing, embracing, committing, caring, and serving. You'll examine this in the next chapter.

Summarizing where you're at in the soul quest helps you identify with any symptoms of soul sickness. There are degrees of urgency and significance to your human condition. You'll find a Spiritual Inventory in chapter eight, which provides a thorough checkup for assessing your spiritual health and well-being. You'll want to wait to explore it until you have read the first seven chapters.

Soul sickness is sometimes mistakenly described as "the loss of will to live." It's only one aspect of the complex spiritual illness exhibited in physical (somatic) complications. Some argue this is a "loss of soul." I beg to differ. Your soul isn't lost; it's hungering for health. Sickness isn't your enemy; it's the angel (messenger) alerting you to act and make changes. God gave breath to your soul, wisdom to your mind, and a spirit guiding you into health and wholeness.

Three

The Health of Your Soul

Everyone is a hunter. Some hunt for love. Some hunt for independence.
Some hunt for truth. Some hunt for serenity. Some hunt for meaning.
Some hunt for hope. Don't ever resent or avoid the hunt. Follow
the hunt wherever it takes you, whatever it makes you.
—From the TV series *Absentia*, Episode 7 (2019)

Have you attempted to resolve your soul's anguish and urgings without success? Do you hunt through book "therapies," surf the internet, or attend lectures by spiritual experts or even psychic readings to find your answers, only to be disappointed? By now, you may have discovered there's no passive means to spiritual health, no magical solutions, and no simplistic approaches to resolving the conflict. There's a fundamental prerequisite to spiritual health—prayer. Some view prayer as a "final act of desperation" when all else fails. This failure to understand the deep meaning of prayer gives no thought to active prayer, which is engaging and interactive and requires the commitment to "act" on what you know and learn. Prayer from the outset is your spiritual chaperone through the pathways to health and wholeness. Prayer doesn't expect an answer to your human condition; it comes from your soul. It connects you to the healing presence and processes of God's Spirit.

One of the dynamics of the Spirit is in the biological nature of all organisms (humans are the most complex). Any organism, no matter how simple or intricate, has tropistic growth. *Tropism* is the natural movement of an organism toward any external stimulus that keeps it alive. It happens when a plant in a dark room approaches any penetrating light; without light, it will soon die.

Many in the medical profession believe every patient has a doctor in them. Healing is the gracious mystery of God's creative order. Any profession in the healing arts is constrained by the self-limiting disorders within the body's healing power range. You're a living organism, not a machine; the difference between the plant and the freedom is choice. The plant has no alternative but to move toward the light. You can accept or reject the Spirit's movement toward life. It's typically referred to as "the will to live" or couched in the Shakespearian question asked by Hamlet: "To be or not to be?" Prayer energizes your body, mind, emotions, and soul to respond to the healing Source of the natural order of creation. Genuine prayer can't be effective when you have been held in bondage to your ego.

Health is native to the human body's need to remain in balance. One's mind, body, and soul are intricately integrated; when disintegration occurs, disease is discovered; whatever affects one part affects the other. None of us is immune to the consequences of mind–body–soul illness. Your wholeness of mind–body–soul breaks down and inevitably succumbs to sickness when you disregard or ignore self-care and nurture. Sickness isn't the enemy; it's the messenger. The word "angel" is translated in Scripture as "messenger." Sickness could be an angel awakening you to the healing presence of God's Spirit. Caring for your body–mind–soul is a sacred trust with God, a covenant as binding as marriage. You must be a good health provider for your body and soul as you are to others. As Paul writes, "Since we have these promises, dear friends, let us purify ourselves from everything that contaminates body and spirit, perfecting holiness out of reverence for God" (2 Cor. 7:1, NIV). Who, not what, is the Spirit? God's creative genius is giving your body–mind–soul limitations. Whenever you go beyond these limits and don't seek balance, you can expect to get tired, depressed, and eventually, physically ill. If your mind–soul can't grasp this reality, your body will. Your entire being lets you know the need for rest, retreat, and relaxation. Sometimes, unfortunately, it takes sickness to hammer this into your brain. Pay attention!

Wholeness is often related to the integrity of the human nervous system required for normal development. This concept also confirms the harmony of any body part functioning with congruity to each other. Sometimes, you may experience life as being out of sync; often, this is signified as sickness or disease. I suggest that wholeness is a quest beckoned by one's soul. It denotes you're open to the surprises, closed doors, and dark alleys of your life as opportunities for experiencing wholeness. The wholeness of self, the wholeness of interpersonal relationships, and the wholeness of meaning and purpose always come in the most unlikely and unexpected places. Wholeness doesn't mean finding completeness, as mentioned previously. Searching for wholeness is a faith process of waiting for, leaping at, discovering, recovering, and experiencing life's endless possibilities. It suggests keeping your soul receptive to God's never-ending grace and being available to the ever-expanding regions of the inner and outer self.

God is always offering wholeness to our splintered existence. The Word of Wholeness invites you to come out of hiding, give up your illusions, and come alive to your full humanity and divinity. Only then can you crawl from the tombs and graves of your own making. You can move from the darkness and dankness of empty living to the fullness and joyfulness of being whole, willing to be filled with God's redeeming love and share fully each day. It's the foundation for holiness known in and through God. Express your commitment by offering the following prayer (you can paraphrase and say it in your own words):

Today, I will open the secret of my soul with no expectations or demands. I will live each moment of this day knowing that anyone or any situation I meet is an opportunity to experience God's holiness and my wholeness. Amen.

Native Americans have deep roots in the natural world. Perhaps all of us should capture the spirit of the tribal peoples. Most American tribes don't celebrate Thanksgiving. They remember the day as a time of mourning. They memorialize the day for the sacrifice their tribes experienced when the Pilgrims arrived. They offer a common prayer when they gather: "Today, we have gathered, and we see that life cycles continue. We have been given the duty to live in balance and harmony with each other and all living things. So now, we bring our minds together as one as we give greetings and thanks to each other as people. Now our minds are one."[10] God created you to be a healthy being. Health is within you. Yet you continually violate the natural laws of health, believing you can escape the inevitable consequences. How deluded can you be? You can't find what you're looking for, going in the wrong direction.

A poignant story illustrates this truth. It was a beautiful fall day; the sky was blue, and six-year-old Tyler was excited to spend time with his father. The outing started at the edge of a forest; the air was filled with the scent of pine and juniper. Tyler had anxiously waited all day for the trip. As Dad unloaded the car, he cautioned Tyler not to wander far: "It's easy to get lost with all of these trees." Tyler was too occupied exploring his surroundings and didn't listen to the warning. He saw a rabbit run past and a squirrel circling a tree. A butterfly landed on a wildflower; a strange noise in the distance caught his ear. Before long, he looked up, and his dad was not in sight. Tyler was afraid, and he took off running and crying for Dad. Tears rolling off his cheeks, he cried, "Daddy! Daddy!" There was only silence.

He was running in circles, the sun setting darkness closing in. He ran until he could run no farther. Suddenly, Tyler heard a familiar voice in the distance: "Tyler! Tyler! Where are you?" He turned; he was lifted quickly into a warm embrace and had his tears wiped away. "Tyler, I kept shouting, but you kept running away. You had to stop running so I could find you."[11] You can't find your way through the forest or wilderness unless you listen to God's Spirit beckoning you to stop going in the direction you're heading; there's another way.

The natural law of health for your body applies to the spiritual well-being of your soul: "For the grace of God has dawned upon the world with healing for all mankind" (Titus 2:11, ESV). The Greek word for "healing" is *soteria*, meaning "salvation." Salvation isn't about the afterlife; it has to do with your daily living. Salvation is delivering your soul from its brokenness. Wholeness (salvation) is the spiritual process of becoming a complete person in the fullness of God's Spirit.

Salvation in English comes from the root word *salvè*, or a healing ointment. Salvation is the healing of the wounds of life. Your wounds are many and profound. When you're deeply wounded, you sense living in a perplexing wilderness. Do you guilelessly run into the wilderness, hoping to escape the pain of your wounds?

Hope for healing recognizes that you're free to be responsive to the healing movement of God's Spirit and live fully (wholly) as God's creation. This freedom of choice means accepting the responsibility for how you live, yet you don't have the freedom to determine the natural and spiritual laws or their outcomes.

You can't continue undermining your patterns of thinking and behaving if you genuinely desire to be physically, emotionally, spiritually, and socially healthy. There's no mystery to living in wellness. No secret diet, therapy, prescription, or religious practice will allow you to ignore health principles and live wholesomely. *Stop it!* Halt whatever you're doing and believing, interrupting God's innate gift of a whole and healthy life. Living disgracefully is to remain in the same old habits, denying God's source of well-being. Grace-filled living affirms, celebrates, and practices wholeness's natural and spiritual laws.

The good news is that the healing ointment of God's grace can sustain you in your most wounded times when you feel most deserted. During those times, you fight with your demons and know you need not be defeated; God's Spirit is with you. Spiritual healing isn't a protection against being wounded or a way to avoid the wilderness moments; it's having a clear and focused mind–soul–spirit that trusts entirely in the promised covenant between God and you; As Jesus claims, "And behold, I am with you always, to the end of the age" (Matt. 28:20, ESV). Here's some wisdom worth remembering. The prophet Kahlil Gibran observed: "Our anxiety does not come from thinking about the future but from wanting to control it."[12]

The following chapters will provide you explicitly with the steps that guide you through the process to spiritual wholeness. I'll admit that limiting your search for spiritual wholeness to twelve steps is unrealistic. Most likely, there are many more steps to take, which are subsets of these steps. However, they are a guide and not a complete process within themselves. In this book, I believe each step escorts your soul quest on an all-encompassing, intensive course. Each step builds on the foundation of the first and the ensuing ones. You'll learn to incorporate each one into your daily routine. Don't causally read through these steps. Reflect on each step and understand the depth of meaning and purpose of the *Twelve Steps to Spiritual Wholeness.*

Four

STEP ONE: SELF-RESPONSIBILITY

We admit we are powerless to change the lives of others, and we will accept the responsibility and consequences of our personal choices.

The beginning of your soul's quest to wholeness is admitting your self-defeating behaviors. Hopefully, you've accepted the undeniable reality regarding that changes to physical health and spiritual well-being only happen when you stop sabotaging yourself. You can't practice unhealthy living patterns and expect wellness. The moment you decide to quit undermining wise, healthy choices will be when your body, mind, and soul naturally move toward health.

Does neediness drive you? Does your self-worth hinge on fixing those who have dependent needs? Are you unwittingly attracted to an individual who you think "needs" you? If so, admit that you like the feeling of taking care of someone with "problems," and your presence seems to make them respond with affection.

You mean well, and your concern is typical when you watch those you love making unhealthy choices and seemingly unaware of how they get into such messes. Emotional detachment is challenging when you're afraid the other person may interpret your response as uncaring or unloving.

On the surface, "caretaking" and "caregiving" appear to be the same. Yet they are contradictions. Are you drawn to those who thrive on you taking care of them? Are they so needy you just won't let go of them for fear they will collapse, and you'll feel guilty?

Caretaking is a compulsive behavior that often is mistaken for love. Your obsessive-compulsive drive keeps you in bondage and instills a sense of power-lessness. It isn't surprising that if you seek help, it's often with someone who's trapped in the same caretaking illusion. This mutual cycle manifests with pro-found emotional and physical draining; your "tank is empty," and you begin turning inward, escaping any contact with others. The opposite of love isn't hate. It's apathy, which means "without suffering." Don't interpret "freedom" as not caring for yourself or anyone else. It's a self-imposed prison, and there's no release. Keep focused as you soon learn how to break this relentless cycle.

As a child, you probably learned, like many, that God created humankind to love others. Unfortunately, this meant "Don't think about yourself"; this is selfish. You developed the belief and carried it into adulthood that "people-pleasing" and "caretaking" are spiritual values at the expense of self-care. You thought self-esteem was determined by caring for others and ignoring your well-being. The truth is that all you must share is your "essence" and "presence."

Love doesn't change someone; ask any spouse or parent of an addict to chemicals, eating disorders, or compulsive behaviors such as gambling, hoard-ing, and so forth. You've no mythical, magical powers to fix those you love. Empathy seems normal when you agonize over the pain your friend or family member is experiencing. Wanting to be supportive is admirable, but God has given each person the inner strength and gifts to deal with personal pain and suffering.

I was in junior high school, and like most teenagers my age, I was vulner-able and susceptible to dynamic, energetic adults who influenced my develop-ing years. I attended a revival with some of my friends in our local church. The evangelist was "on fire;" I listened closely to every word. At the end of the service, he invited anyone ready to give their life to God to join him at the altar. One of my best friends got up and walked down the aisle; he turned and motioned me to follow him. I stood; my feet felt like dried concrete, and I couldn't move. My friend came, took my arm, and pulled me to the altar; I knelt with a thud, clinging to the rail to keep from falling. I had no clue what "giving my life to God" meant, yet I looked up; the evangelist seemed to examine my heart and soul. I knew I wasn't ready to be a preacher, so why was I here?

The voice of the fiery preacher suddenly became soft, almost a whisper, and I heard what I thought he said: "God has invited you to this moment to accept your commitment to celebrate the gift of your life; God birthed you into this time in history to affirm your birthright as a chosen one personally." My mind instantly wandered and wondered what being "chosen" meant. Had I naively, unintentionally decided against my will? How would my life be different knowing I had been "elected"? My eyes opened, and the minister's words caught my ears as he explained, "Everyone is a chosen child of God, but not everyone is willing to be one since these demands becoming responsible for your life." I learned that God doesn't "take care" of you; giving your life to God is returned to your keeping and accountability. God's Spirit is your source of strength and guidance, not some "Holy Protector." Your life's yours; no one can live it for you. God didn't create us to be helpless victims of this world; your mind–soul–spirit is empowered to confront the ups and downs of everyday life.

You can learn defense mechanisms and coping skills to resolve inner and outer conflicts. The power of decision-making doesn't promise you'll continuously make the right choice, only that you dare to act and be responsible for the outcome. A new day allows you to make an informed decision; being "chosen" charges you to make wise choices gained through spiritual discernment. You recognize your inability to make choices or decisions for others, no matter how much you want. I could easily have "blamed" my friend for "pulling" me to the altar that night. Later, I realized it was God tugging at my heart to decide to get on with my life rather than waiting for someone or something to tell me what I needed to do or be. Living a responsible life is a burden and blessing. Yet you grow deeper in understanding, compassion, identification, and recognition when created to be in a community with other "chosen ones."

When you spend time and energy rescuing others, you reinforce the low self-esteem of those you're trying to help. Your enabling behavior may be seen as caring; in reality, you're inflating your ego and deflating the worth of others. It's undermining the ability of the "victim" to become capable and responsible for their own life.

Discovering God's gift of personal responsibility is an unfathomable truth. It's also frightening that you'll find it difficult to accept much less practice. Self-responsibility isn't negating others or its unwillingness to help others in need. The more you love and care for others, the more your self-love is grounded. Self-responsibility doesn't happen in isolation. We're social beings, and therefore, our actions do impact others. Freedom to make decisions requires you to accept the consequences of your choices. Who doesn't want to pass on the responsibility of life sometime? There are moments when it seems appealing to turn over all my problems and decisions to someone else. Certain individuals have told me you *must* "turn your life and problems over to God. God will take care of you." What a great concept! Or is it? Does this approach mean God is taking accountability and responsibility for my life?

Certainly, God provides guidance, insight, and strength for our human struggles. Yet God has given each of us the freedom to make choices, and with this freedom comes the responsibility of accepting the consequences of our decisions. God is a *permitting* (healthy) power, not a *restricting* one. When you give up responsibility for your life in any dimension, you become disabled and fall victim to helplessness and despair.

You need an open heart–soul–mind, searching for and being led by God's Spirit. You can discover wisdom and awareness through prayerful attending to God's presence, but God won't release you from the awesome responsibility of living and accepting the consequences; this isn't a burden, but a redemptive blessing.

One of life's givens is how accountability and responsibility are attached, so you can't separate them. Even more complicated is that you can't discover your authentic self until you balance these two principles. You're liable for taking the faith journey and accommodating all the trials, tribulations, and triumphs on this eventful venture called life. You're responsible *to* others, not *for* others.

When President Obama gave his first inaugural address, his voice in crescendo called our nation "a new era of responsibility!" What did he mean? As citizens of this great country, we must stop blaming others for the consequences of hate, violence, and social isolation from one another. Everyone must take ownership of their decisions or be unwilling to make them. You can't live in a vacuum nor be so entangled in the lives of others that everyone feels helpless and powerless.

Jesus altered the perspective of the invalid at the pool of Bethesda. He hopefully kept waiting for someone to lift him into the healing waters. Jesus boldly said, "Get up. Pick up your mat and walk" (John 5:8, NIV). Today's version could read, "Pick up your life and live it!" No one else can do it for you.

Self-responsibility is a learned process; you aren't born with this social skill. You're born dependent on the needs of care from your parents (or surrogate parents). An infant relies on the nurturing and supportive attention required for healthy growth. Along the way, the effective parent or guardian begins to teach and practice "detachment," and the emotional/spiritual umbilical cord is gradually severed; by adolescence, you start "rebelling" or "complying," depending on your response to the experience of maturing.

If you were a rebel, you refused to develop the skill of responsibility. You blamed others for your circumstances in life. You refused to respect authority and claimed to be your "boss." Most likely, you wouldn't read a book that encourages and gives guidelines to self-responsibility unless you're weary from the "demons" that possess you; you're exhausted from the constant battle of combating the enemies who seem to keep you hostage.

The other typical response to your developmental years was to create a person of compliance; you gave your power to those who told you how to live, what to do, and how to act. You became a "people pleaser," always seeking acceptance, approval, affirmation, and recognition from others. When your actions fail to achieve desired outcomes, your stomach gets in a knot, and anger is repressed, eventually leading to depression. You fear taking risks or making a personal decision for fear of failure or disappointing others.

Acting and moving forward always begins with releasing the past and letting go of all the baggage that keeps you stuck. It's where your life-changing journey is launched. There's no looking back. In some psychotherapy, even psychoanalysis, a therapist discourages self-responsibility; these models focus on the past and present. Self-responsibility in this book emphasizes moving into your future rather than rehashing or rehearsing your past.

Healthy self-responsibility doesn't ignore or discount your past behaviors, but you learn the "positive intentions" that motivate the behavior. No matter how unhealthy, all behavior has a logical reason. Now, your worldview initiates the logic, not someone else's perception. Affirming your positive intention validates the value and belief, prompting a particular action. Believing you're helping someone you love without the intention of hurting or disappointing someone is understandable. Your desire to affirm someone's value and worth is noble. However, sometimes your engagement with another won't always be understood or appreciated. They may even interpret your actions as reinforcing self-negating feelings in them. You intend to care, but your behavior becomes taking care of, which isn't your desire. Effective self-responsibility exhibits for others how to care for themselves. Internal affirmation doesn't seek approval from others. Caring is its own reward; the value or importance of caring is "caring."

Once you recognize your power, you'll be amazed by the weight lifted from foolishly giving your "power" away. Living your life becomes a blessing, and you discover inner peace. Those you love and care for (not take care of) are blessed by your presence in their lives.

Self-responsibility is attentive to the body messages informing you of the stressors that take their levy on your complete health. You develop an awareness and sensitivity to how you create stress triggered by myths and perceptions that are unhealthy and fabricated. God's Spirit empowers you to break the chains that bind you and keep you locked in a prison of your own. It's also true that others close to you probably have reinforced this cavern and confirmed your worst self-portrait. It happens whenever you give your power away. God gives you the capabilities and resources to manage, even change, stressors to discover new self-care choices and care for others.

Scripture has many positive affirmations about self-care and self-worth. Keep focused on the following texts as insightful:

Beloved, I pray that all may go well with you and that you
may be in good health, as it goes well with your soul.
—3 John 1:2, ESV

I can do all things through him who strengthens me.
—Philippians 4:13, ESV

*For you formed my inward parts; you knitted me together in my
mother's womb. I praise you, for I am fearfully and wonderfully
well. Wonderful are your works; my soul knows it very well.*
—Psalm 139:13–14, ESV

Step One establishes the context vital to everything you learn in your soul quest. Developing self-responsibility and self-care will test your mental, emotional, physical, and spiritual strength. Self-will and determination must be maximized. Thich Nhat Hanh, a world-renowned Zen master and Vietnamese monk, is a walking testament to spiritual wholeness. His quiet manner doesn't overshadow an unfathomable, intense commitment to love and investment in the transformation of humanity. He instilled an appreciation for accepting every twenty-four hours as a divine gift: "Never let a day pass without breathing in the beauty of life without denying the human tragedy. Develop an inner vision of the outer world that recognizes possibilities, not limitations."[13]

Five

STEP TWO: EMPOWERED TO GROW

*We believe and will trust in a creative and interactive God who
can restore us to spiritual wholeness and empower us to grow.*

I'm convinced you have often used two words—belief and trust—in conversations with different people; probably, you interchanged those words, thinking they were synonymous. While this isn't typically a problem, it becomes one when you want to define your *beliefs* regarding the *spiritual principles* that guide your spirit and soul. I hope you'll understand and accept that these familiar words are two sides of the same coin known as *faith*.

Faith can't survive in a culture of apathy or indifference. Apathy has no interest or concern about God. This indifference contributes significantly to unwellness in the world and at home. Sickness isn't the loss of wellness; it's the activity of practicing unwell behaviors. You may be treated for an illness, and the symptoms are resolved, but this doesn't mean you're now well or healthy. Health and wellness require proactive measures resulting in interaction with God's Spirit and the natural healing order.

Step Two is an inclusive practice of verifying a positive affirmation about the God of your understanding. Belief is *knowing* what you accept as accurate or fact. Trust is *acting* on what you believe. You may think there's a God, but this has no manifestation in how you live or act. Your words and behavior give no credence to living a spiritual life, especially a healthy one.

The second step is yielding to your soul quest by working on faith to transport you into the unknown, uncharted waters of authentic wellness. Faith links the distressed parts of your life with the Spirit's healing touch. Faith allows you to become so intimately connected to God that the Creator's wholeness becomes your wholeness.

The late Dr. Sidney Jourard, a clinical psychologist, claims that "all healing involves faith." He continues by stating that faith isn't a guarantee of a cure; it's keeping our inner spirit and human organism open to all the mysterious powers and possibilities of healing.[14]

Theologian John Cobb Jr. rightly questions, "Would it be better to maintain, in the face of all contrary probabilities, an attitude of utter confidence that whatever we ask of God he will give us? Surely not! If we want to move mountains, we had better stick to bulldozers."[15] It's a perversion of God's Truth to suppose that the person who dies of cancer suffers from a lack of faith. Remember, Saint Paul asked three times that his affliction be removed, which wasn't done (2 Cor. 12:7, NIV). Helen Keller's sight and hearing were never restored. Yet she discovered how to live with the mystery of her condition and realized new possibilities in life.

In Jon Kabat-Zinn's book *Wherever You Go There You Are*, he has a chapter called "Interconnectedness." In it, he tells the tale of a fox that drinks most of an older woman's milk pail. The woman cuts off the fox's tail in a fit of anger. She tells the fox his tail won't be restored until her milk is replaced. He faced a daunting task before this could happen. He searches for a cow, a maiden, and a stream for water, and finally, he meets a kind miller who helps the fox get everything he needs to fill the elderly lady's milk pail and get his tail back. The author explains the story: "Nothing comes from nothing. Everything has its antecedents. What we call life, or health, or the biospheres are all complex systems of interconnections."[16]

Faith functions in all the "complex systems of interconnections." Your health and well-being will be transformed in ways you never imagined or thought possible. Prayer and faith are prerequisites in the realization of wholeness.

Her eyes were as wide as a full moon, her heart racing like an engine warming up, tiptoeing as if a mime in slow motion; magic was in her grasp, but she didn't dare touch it. The mystery of life was happening in her presence, and each breath was exhaled with awe, a grin as big as a circus clown. Then it opened from what seemed to be a rolled leaf; a rainbow of color in the shape of a butterfly struggles to freedom. Life begins again, the mystery of all mysteries: birth, death, and rebirth.

Emerging from the cocoon is a solitary passage. In the darkness, you struggle to be free, fighting to be released. You become stronger, strengthened for the new life and prepared for a fresh adventure.

You've been given the gift of life as a fiduciary trust. You're answerable to God for your investments and returns on this gift. You can't surrender the sacred trust you're granted without violating the gift and the Giver.

It's said that you fear what you don't understand. Emancipating your fears means breaking free from mistaken beliefs. Identify your relationship creeds and values. Are they valid, or do they hold "magical" powers over your behavior? Check out their reality or the importance they've been to you. You can't form healthy beliefs unless you escape the faulty influence your "old" beliefs have in keeping you trapped in debilitating patterns of relating to others. These beliefs have become emotional and behavioral habits that appear to be automatic. Listen! Such beliefs don't define you.

Discerning the difference between "feeling" a belief and "knowing" a belief is critical. In your early, developing years, what you learn about life is mostly feelings associated with your actions. When you do nice things for others, you will feel better. When you disappoint others, you feel bad. What a *lie*!

Feelings have no moral value; feelings are feelings and can't be controlled by changing your behavior. Accept your feelings, whether positive or negative. Learning self-responsibility is recognizing how dysfunctional beliefs have shaped your codependent behavior.

The *Merriam-Webster Dictionary* defines "dysfunctional" as "impaired or abnormal functioning; abnormal or unhealthy interpersonal behavior or interaction within a group. Belief is described as a conviction of the truth of some statement or the reality of some being or phenomenon, especially when based on an examination of evidence."[17]

These two descriptions seem sterile and complicated. Trying to grasp the whole meaning of harmful beliefs may seem impossible, and the more veiled they are, the more risk they pose to your emotional, mental, and physical health.

On the surface, a dysfunctional belief appears rational, giving you the strength to act without considering self-interest. You didn't adopt this belief, thinking it was harmful, until now when you reflect on the costs you have paid personally. Changing these beliefs to ones that foster positive attitudes and actions for developing an interdependent self-concept will be rewarding.

Your old beliefs are built on distortions of reality. Here are some of the untruths, which are called cognitive distortions. Such distortions interfere with accurately perceiving and feeling an interaction or event. Below is a brief review of some belief distortions:

Absolute thinking: You identify your world in black and white, with no place for gray. Your vocabulary uses words like *always, never, everywhere, no doubt,* and so forth to describe a situation or person. You won't admit to a fallacy of interpretation of what you experience.

Hasty generalizations: Conclusions that are made on insufficient or biased evidence. When you've experienced failure or discomfort in a particular situation, you determine this will happen in similar circumstances. You've had a conflicting encounter with someone of another race, sex, or religious faith, giving you the impression that anyone like them will act accordingly.

Filtering: You tend to ignore or filter any information or experience that fails to conform to your narrow beliefs. If given a compliment or affirmation, you refuse to accept it because your brain blocks the "truth" of these comments. You probably interpret what you hear as hidden criticisms rather than words of encouragement. You focus on what isn't said or excuse it as naivete without knowing your self-concept.

Discounting: Anyone who tries to show positive care is seen as manipulative and not genuine. You believe you aren't worthy of this attention, certainly not deserving. You've formed a belief system that holds fast to diminished self-worth and an inability to accept accomplishments. You cling to others for your identity, and those individuals discount your efforts to help others, much less yourself. The problem for you is how you migrate toward such people who reinforce your negative self-image.

Mind reading: You believe you know what someone is thinking or feeling. You trust your intuition and don't accept what someone is saying or how you react irrationally. You even tell someone that you know her better than she knows herself. It's the magnification of your control over others. Don't be surprised when healthy people ignore or avoid you!

Take time to learn about other cognitive distortions where you've habitually acted irrationally. Allow your mind to be open to discoveries that will expand your world of reality. Displace biases, mythical thinking, ignorance, and childish thoughts with authentic and reliable truths (tenets).

Let's review other aspects of the Second Step. The phrase "creative and interactive God" is so comprehensive (theological and philosophical giants have written volumes) that I'm presenting the initial meaning of what I've learned through my professional and educational background rooted in personal experience.

Creative and *interactive* are words of action describing the God of creation with vitality and the desire to communicate. God not only *"created"* but is continually involved in the creative evolvement of all creation, human and otherwise. God isn't finished with us or civilization. Your life, my life, and everyone's lives are emerging, and God's Spirit interacts and prompts our actions. Living isn't a set of rigid beliefs or frigid feelings. God isn't in the gaps (the unexplainable) or the mysterious; instead, God's in every place filled with desolation and richness, emptiness, and fullness.

Humboldt's Gift, the powerful book by Pulitzer Prize–winning Saul Bellow, gives voice to one of his characters, Citrine, saying to an optimistic friend, "The disorder is here to stay. I keep living with the illusion that someday, all the puzzle pieces of my life will fit neatly together. No more enigmas! No more unwanted surprises! No more uninvited intrusions! No unexpected pain!"[18]

The disorder isn't chaos or futility; neither is it the outcry of depression or failure. I had to learn how to admit that my life, at times, is absurd and a puzzle. I needed to rely on a creative and interactive God whose empowering

Spirit is ever-present in my questions and misgivings about me and my whole world.

Faith is interactive and responds trustingly to the ever-changing events of life; it makes no demand for order. You flow with the movements of each day, knowing that God's wisdom and direction undergird your daily experiences.

While it's sometimes appropriate to plan, you must also make allowances for interruptions, unscheduled visitors, and sudden shifts in priorities. Living by faith and spiritual strength means being flexible enough to let go of your unbending schedules and answer the moment's needs.

You need to stay in control and keep things running smoothly and will find the skill of flexibility challenging and your susceptibility rather dubious to *faith*. Nevertheless, faith is the only constant that secures you amid disorder. You're empowered by faith, so do you dare to risk it today?

Step Two confirms that you're filled with possibilities beyond your limited perceptions and convictions. You're not what you have done in the past; you are becoming who God created you to be. It's why we ask to "be restored to spiritual wholeness."

Restoration is the recognition that God has created (birthed) you with spiritual wholeness, and you have violated the essence of your "whole" being. You aren't in search of God but acknowledging God's search for you. It's why Jesus tells the Prodigal Son's parable (Luke 15:11–32, ESV). The son takes his inheritance and leaves home to find his purpose and identity in the "world." After squandering everything and himself, the young man comes to his senses and realizes all his "worldly" living has brought him emptiness and loneliness; he anxiously returns home. What a surprise to discover his father comes running to meet him and welcome him home. The father had always anticipated the reunion with his lost son, feeling assured that their relationship would be restored.

Wholeness is about aligning perfectly with your identity, your authentic self with God's Spirit. Your mind, soul, and spirit yearn for "fulfillment" rather than "happiness." You become fully synchronized with the inner and outer world. Wholeness is the fullest expression of wonder and possibility.

Prayer for Today

God, give me the inner peace and outer vision to live each moment of this day with the exciting possibilities of the unknown and unplanned. Help me release the control I need over my life and the people around me so I can discover the freedom of Your Living Presence. Amen.

Six

STEP THREE: SPIRITUAL GUIDANCE

*We freely respond to God's spiritual guidance and faithfully act
upon the decisions we make through spiritual discernment.*

My assessment of the soul quest or resurgence of spirituality is observable today by countless people looking for any good news that will promise self-affirmation, seekers wanting a spiritual guru telling them everything will be all right. Through the years, I've received promotional mailings from spiritual sages, offering me a weekend of an in-depth discovery of my inner self and connecting it to the Cosmic Soul. They pledge I can learn to feel good about myself and reclaim *me*.

Some religious experts are preaching a message of the New Great Awakening. We live in a time of spiritual turmoil and spiritual hunger, a stage of digging into the fundamental values of the past to provide some anchoring for the unknown ahead. What's dissimilar about this awakening is there's little agreement on the source or Who or What God is, who defines you, or me. Instead, this path is your pursuit of knowing God and committing to a covenantal relationship through continual spiritual guidance and spiritual discernment.

You now begin walking the path of Step Three. You'll learn and practice specific spiritual disciplines. Discipline requires determination and constant attention. There's no space for hesitation or apology for personal inadequacies. You're not using intuition or guessing to make decisions. Spiritual guidance and spiritual discernment are distinct functions and skills. Decision-making keeps a balance between "guidance" and "discernment." Whenever you change an old way of life, the disappearance of old patterns and old ways of doing things, and move toward something new, you live in visionary times; there's uncertainty in your daily activities. You want guidance in the responses you need to make. Realize and affirm that God is birthing something new in you, around you, and beyond you.

Spiritual guidance: Paul reminds the Christians at Philippi of this truth: "For it is God who is at work in you, enabling you both to will and work for God's good pleasure" (Phil. 2:13, NIV). Spiritual guidance ultimately involves inner wisdom and distinguishing truth from error (false teachings). It's perceived and sensed as "rightness," accompanied by a calming of your soul. It's your quiet, inner space grounded in, centered on, and guided by the working of the Holy Spirit with your spirit. The clamoring of outside voices often drowns out the internal communication you want with God's Spirit. The familiar words of the Psalmist echo the divine voice: "Be still and know that I am God" (Ps. 46:10, NIV).

In the fourth and fifth centuries, the Desert Fathers made expeditions into the desert (remote places), where they weren't disturbed; they fled the cities to escape the chaos and interruptions of the social environment. These mystics had deep longings for connection with the Holy and Sacred. The Fathers, like you, learned and practiced spiritual guidance.

Locate your space for solace and solitude without any of the trappings that can clutter your mind, soul, and spirit. You don't need to retreat to the desert but to a place where you sense a sacred silence. Don't bring tarot cards, Ouija board, crystals, and so forth. Spiritual guidance doesn't include physical objects as a means for listening to God's Spirit. I don't encourage a musical backdrop or guided imagery at this point in your journey. I'm not dismissing the importance of the Holy Scriptures and divinely inspired writings of spiritually mature teachers—that is, Buddha, Mohammed, the Dalai Lama, Gandhi, Mother Teresa, Saint Francis, and many more. They have value for your quest; however, we're beginning with spiritual guidance from the One who breathed life into your lungs and being.

Recognizing and following God's spiritual guidance will be your daily challenge. But first, you must develop a frame of reference regarding understanding God's will for your life. It's grounded in your decisions and actions in the real world of relationships between yourself and others.

Your soul is to be sensitive and responsive to God's Spirit. It's connected intrinsically to your heart. In many religious traditions, the heart is the vital organ that gives life to the human body; without a functioning heart, the body dies. The heart in the spiritual realm embraces understanding and insight. Your soul and spirit mutually communicate with the sincere desire to make decisions and act on what "feels right" and brings "inner peace." You don't feel like there is any conflict with your total being. It's not about feeling confident and sure about your choices or decisions but a willingness to act on what you discern regarding God's will for your life. Some theologians call this "being spiritually minded." It's a matter of life and death. Paul said in Romans 8:6 (ESV), "For to set the mind on the flesh is death, but to set the mind on the Spirit is life and peace." Spiritual-mindedness sees all of life with a God-consciousness. You're born spiritually oriented. Everyone has their way of spiritual discernment. No two people emerge from their sacred practices with the same outcomes. You need to feel open and responsive to your spirit's connection to God's Spirit. You want to feel safe and comfortable. The following guidelines are to be free-flowing, not a rigid ritual.

Spiritual centering: In this world of confusion and vast division, you may feel splintered in many ways. You most likely feel pulled in various directions with little sense of who you are and where you are going. Finding your "center" seems impossible, perhaps unlikely. However, you don't *do* centering; it's a significant process in experiencing wholeness or integration. It's the means of distancing your body, mind, and soul inwardly from outer influences that continually force you to live in a schizoid world. As a result, you realize being between the mountains and valleys of life happenings, and you're protected.

In the Judeo-Christian tradition, we must trust the Creator God, who provides guidance and strength for our life journey. The story of Moses leading his people to the Promised Land demonstrates this reality. Moses reminds the journeyers that it's difficult. Among them are doubters and unbelievers who question where they're going and when they will see God's promise fulfilled.

He assures his kindred followers they've nothing to fear (or doubt), for God goes before them every step of the way (Deut. 1:29–33, KJV).

You'll discover that life's gift fills you with adventure and unimaginable possibilities. Your journey begins inwardly and is fully reached outwardly, where you're engaged fully in an Awakening. One of the most important things in life is spiritual centering. It involves a personal philosophy of life.

Your spiritual center is a mystical place within yourself where you achieve mental, physical, and emotional peace, even for a short period. Even if you aren't religious, your spirituality is how you care for yourself and others. *Centering* is an intentional practice beginning with your attention on the present, not the past or future. Now is the only time that matters.

When your mind-soul is stuck with feelings and attitudes of anger, depression, loneliness, guilt, shame, and so forth, you need to learn how to release the energy invested in this personal world of negativity. Paul warns us: "Do not conform any longer to the pattern of this world but be transformed by the renewing of your mind" (Rom. 12:2, NIV).

Typically, those who measure and compare themselves to others have low self-esteem. Your identity isn't affirming your self-worth. You focus on your inadequacies, limitations, inabilities, or failures, never feeling equal in most relationships. Your personal needs aren't being met. You respond in one of two unhealthy ways. If your needs growing up were unmet or dismissed, you tend to withdraw, or you discount your needs or believe they can't be met. You fall into fantasies or make-believe. You withdraw, falsely discovering books, music, movies, television, social media, and drugs provide the illusion of being all right. You become timid and powerless and don't trust anyone.

The other alternative is overcompensating with hostile obstinacy of anger, self-indulgence, abusive relationships, denial, and addictions. You collect friendships as fodder to fulfill *your* needs. You quickly discard anyone who can't or won't service your selfishness! Delusions distort reality, and your worldview becomes absolute. Mental, emotional, and spiritual health are foreign views impossible to experience.

Working and practicing the steps to holistic health can explode and implode everything you think, believe, or have experienced. You're learning how to discover a new way of living. *Centering is the avenue to self-care.* Change begins through the active presence of God's Spirit. You experience this truth in the moments or occasions when you're inspired and encouraged to find a more meaningful and happier life.

Inspiring is associated with many dimensions of life, such as music, writing, painting, acting, orating, and so forth. It's the process of being mentally stimulated to do or feel something, especially to do something creative. In religion or spirituality, inspiration is the divine influence of God's Spirit. Claiming this truth for your life requires the hunger to change from within, but the power you need to change is only made available through the work of the Holy Spirit: "It is God who works in you, both to will and to work for his good pleasure" (Phil. 2:13, ESV).

How does the Spirit's inspiration guide you toward spiritual health? Accepting that your self-defeating habits and beliefs prevent spiritual wholeness would be best. For example, you have negative, persistent thoughts and actions reinforcing your sense of worthlessness. Or you overplay with an attitude of arrogance, attempting to act and be self-centered with feelings of superiority.

Then, you need to genuinely seek the personal power or potential to discover your new life. Caution! After years of negativity and self-doubt, accepting a new truth about yourself can feel frightening. You may be tempted not to believe this is possible. Don't give up when inspiration is hard and change doesn't look promising. The Apostle Paul faced many trials and suffering, yet he encouraged his followers, "Let us not grow weary of doing good, for in due season we will reap if we do not give up" (Gal. 6:9, NIV).

Inspiration in our current dialogue is not a search for creativity but a quest for personal transformation. This discovery occurs when divine guidance encourages, motivates, visualizes, influences, and guides you into a new awareness of self-worth and fresh beginnings. God's Spirit initially guides you to repentance. It happens when you take an inventory of your past life. Subsequently, admit (confess) to the self-destructive, unhealthy thoughts or behaviors that kept you on the dark side of life.

The Greek word for repent is *metanoia*, signifying "change your mind." You may tend to fluctuate; you aren't sure what to consider. One moment, you think a certain way and suddenly flip to an opposite idea. There's little consistency in your thoughts or actions. Repentance acts courageously to make committed decisions, firmness, and strength of mind.

Paul faced this problem with some members of the church in Rome: "Do not be conformed to this world but be transformed by the renewing of your mind" through the power of God's Spirit" (Rom. 12:1–2, ESV). It's essential to understand the significance and power of repentance. You need to expand or even change your belief regarding the nature and capacity of God. God is relational.

God is the Creator of all life, yet the creation story was incomplete until Adam and Eve awakened in the Garden of Eden. God sought companionship. Even when Eve tempted Adam to eat from the Tree of Knowledge, they became aware of their nakedness and covered their bodies. God wasn't pleased with their disobedience.

God didn't cast them from the Garden as a punishment but as a sign that their knowledge now made them responsible for themselves. God gave them the remarkable gift of freedom to choose from the challenging tasks of being caretakers of this sacred world beyond the Garden of Innocence.

We learn from the biblical story that God is love, and from the beginning of time, God establishes a loving relationship with all creation, especially with Adam and Eve. God doesn't judge nor punish anyone. We discover with the Psalmist, "Make a joyful shout to the Lord, all you land!…The joy of the Lord is my strength" (Ps. 100:1, KJV). Psalm 16:11 (KJV) says, "You will show me the path of life. In Your presence is fullness of joy; at Your right hand are pleasures forever." He also reminds us, "Weeping may endure for a night, but joy comes in the morning" (Ps. 30:5b, KJV).

These biblical verses underscore Open Relational Theology's teachings that claim an uncontrollable God acts with uncontrollable love. There can be no other option in God's wisdom to endow humankind with free choice. Otherwise, freedom without responsibilities is a sham. We need not repent or ask forgiveness if God is the absolute controller. It would be like an unhealthy, misguided, and controlling parent using love to manipulate the attitude and behavior of a child.

Many people have distorted views of God's nature and character. Often, their perceptions mirror the parents they experienced growing up or the adults and parents seen daily through them. These personal happenings shape God as an omnipotent, all-powerful being who has predetermined our destinies. This image believes God determines our path, but our ability to decide has limitations. There are consequences for each decision we make.

Your spiritual map narrows the possibilities of an intimate God who loves and forgives you unconditionally. God grieves in your suffering and strengthens you in times of trouble. It gives you joy when experiencing celebrations or gratitude for countless blessings.

All of us are inclined to be ungrateful, disobedient, selfish, arrogant, and even stubborn. God's grace is the source of forgiveness through the Divine Spirit's gift of repentance. Repentance restores your broken relationship (which is the true meaning of "sin") with God and others. How does this work?

Repentance involves recognizing that your attitudes, behaviors, thoughts, spiritual anemia, and relationships are filled with emptiness, hostilities, and the sense that you're unlovable or incapable of loving others. You awaken from this painful reality and admit to yourself and God that your misery is self-defeating and depressing. They're feeling overwhelmed with guilt and shame. Coping with shame is like viewing life through smashed glasses. Blurring vision, shadowy sights. Cracked windows with distorted views.

Repentance is an avenue to spiritual health. You'll discover a spiritual vibrancy you have longed to desire. However, being confined to the secrecy of deficiency, anger, or withdrawal can be frightening. Guilt and shame are bound to each other. Guilt's focus is on remorse for disturbing behaviors or actions. Shame centers on your self-identity as being worthless or useless.

What's true regarding guilt and shame as connected is also valid for repentance and forgiveness. The process of shame is a learned response, and it is not natural. Guilt is the emotional reaction evolving from shameful criticism. It's taught, not caught. John Steinbeck, a genius author, was often a brutal observer of humanity. He wrote, "It is true that we are weak and sick and ugly and quarrelsome, but if that is all we ever were, we would millenniums ago have disappeared from the face of the earth."[19]

Repentance is a spiritual practice inviting you to a new life. When Jesus started his public ministry, he called for repentance. Matthew 4:17 (ESV) records, "From that time on Jesus began to preach, 'Repent, for the kingdom of heaven has come near.'" Jesus speaks of repentance: "I tell you that in the same way, there will be more rejoicing in heaven over one sinner who repents than over ninety-nine righteous persons who do not need to repent" (Luke 15:7, ESV).

Jesus, the Redeemer, talked about a change of heart toward ourselves, the world, and God, an inner change that gives rise to new ways of living. Genuine repentance is an inner change of heart that produces the fruits of new behavior. These fruits of the spirit are in Galatians 5:22–23 (NIV), where the Apostle Paul says, "But the fruit of the Spirit is love, joy, peace, longsuffering, kindness, goodness, faithfulness, gentleness, self-control." Repentance sets you free. You aren't a slave kept in bondage. Addictions and rigid actions control your mind, soul, and heart. As suggested previously, your inner voice has deafened God's Spirit. Walt Kelly's political cartoon satire of Pogo gave him the most quoted cliché: "We have met the enemy, and he is us."

However, God doesn't see us as "enemies" who require transformation. Instead, we are "children" with broken minds, hearts, and souls needing healing and restoration. God waits for us to initiate this possibility. So where do you begin?

It's not a shame game. God didn't create you to be perfect. However, confessing your brokenness and grief regarding the anger, hate, abuse, neglect, and punishment of self and others can be "gut-wrenching." Unless you're troubled by your attitudes, feelings, and behaviors toward yourself and others, you'll continue to be a prisoner of your own making. Go to a quiet (no music, books, television, food, etcetera), meditative (silent) place. Start recognizing and accepting this will be an uncomfortable process. You have the courage and willingness to walk this spiritual quest. God's Spirit will guide you.

Repentance is a balance between confession and forgiveness. Confession involves "godly grief." It's the experience of your actions toward others. Penance or repentance is required. You get consumed with remorse, obsessing over the anguish inflicted on those you love and hate. Worldly grief seeks compensation and restitution. This type of grief drives you to a "get even" posture. Somebody should be punished for their evil ways. Unfortunately, you're the most hated enemy (according to Pogo).

Paul reminds us of the outcomes of worldly grief versus godly grief:

Distress (grief) that drives us to God does that. It turns us around. It gets us back in the way of salvation. We never regret that kind of pain. But those who let distress drive them away from God are full of regrets and end up on a deathbed of regrets. And now, isn't it wonderful all the ways in which this distress has goaded you closer to God? You're more alive, more concerned, more sensitive, more reverent, more human, more passionate, and more responsible. Looked at from any angle, you've come out of this with the purity of heart. (2 Cor. 7:10–11, *MSG*.)

It's your time for healing. God's spirit is moving you toward reconciliation and redemption. A beautiful invitation to a new life awaits you. But are you committed to your quest? You walk into a new day filled with possibilities, so cherish every moment that God gives you! Are you ready?

The profound joy of forgiveness will kindle warmth in your heart and soul. Forgiveness is reciprocal, meaning you are inspired to forgive others as you accept God's forgiveness. The Lord's Prayer includes the warning, "Forgive us our trespasses [sins] as we forgive those who trespass [sinned] against us" (Matt. 6:9–13, ESV).

Accepting God's forgiveness is a blessing. Your ability to compassionately forgive those who have hurt, harmed, cursed, or ignored you requires emptying all the resentments and suffering. Yet this isn't a demand or expectation from God. Forgiveness is an act of God's unconditional grace. The principle of forgiveness is built on mercy. Forgiveness is about humility, not humiliation. Instead of a closed fist ready to fight anyone in your way, you offer open hands for warmth and solace. A forgiving heart is a giving heart. It's a pure heart. It's an empty heart anxiously seeking to be filled with God's goodness. God can only fill an empty heart. You've filled your heart and mind with bitterness, sadness, loathing, and distancing yourself from loved ones for many years. As a result, your heart and soul have become diseased. Hopefully, you are discovering God's love and hope for your life.

How do you tell the difference between self-centered interests and God's desire for you to be a soul-directed, heart-filled, and servant-led person? Whose voice is your decision-making guide? I suggest society's healthy mantra should be, "Take care of yourself. If you don't, who will?" Today, the "Me Too" movement is gaining momentum in contrast to the "We" mentality. Me Too rightfully is confronting the sexual abuse and demeaning of women in our day. However, God seeks inclusiveness of all (*We*).

What's the difference between self-deception, social or political misconception, or rigid tradition often cluttered with significant distortions? Many religious teachings harbor pathological beliefs and practices. My tradition, Christianity, isn't exempt! So how do any of us deal with this conflict? Discover and exercise "spiritual discernment."

Spiritual discernment is the purposeful practice by which a community or an individual seeks, recognizes, and intentionally takes part in the activity of God in everyday settings. Your decisions and guidance happen in the presence of God's Spirit, who warmly cares about you and lets you participate in the divine pursuits of restoration and revolution. The concern is accepting God's spiritual guidance by making grace-filled decisions (free from self-sabotage) and relating to and treating others daily with compassion, acceptance, forgiveness, and supportive care. Be aware! No method guarantees how the spirit is discerned because the Holy Spirit can't be captured in a formula. But you can learn ways to practice discernment that helps counter self-deception and heighten the possibility that God's Spirit can be known.

Be wary of anyone who claims, "God told me to do this!" Paul had the same concern when speaking to the church in Thessalonica: "Do not quench the Spirit. Do not treat prophecies with contempt but test them all; hold on to what is good" (1 Thess. 5:19–21, NIV). Saint John agrees with Paul: "Belove, believe not every spirit, but prove the spirits, whether they are of God; because many false prophets are gone out into the world" (John 4:1, ESV).

You're not expected to be a prophet, much less a saint. Spiritual health and wholeness are an invitation to share and witness God's healing power in this time of your life. You've been given this life in God's majestic creation. To celebrate the wonder of who you are, not the false or distorted image of your past. One metaphor expresses how your life needs to be lived: "Your life is much like an echo. What you send out comes back to you. If you send love,

love returns to you. If you send anger and resentment, do not be surprised when hostility bounces back!"[20]

Discernment responds to spiritual standards or ethical principles disclosed through God's Spirit. You or others aren't the authority or ground of personal decisions. The truth, wisdom, and inspiration of an uncontrolling God guide your soul, mind, heart, and body. Don't blame God. You're responsible for the "echoes" you send to others. So you can be an echo (voice) of God's Spirit.

Discover your uniqueness. Don't mimic those you admire or accept their principles or values. Paul reminds his fellow disciples in Ephesus: "Everything you are and think and do is permeated (saturated) with Oneness (unity). But that doesn't mean you should all look and speak and act the same. Out of the generosity of Christ (Holy Presence), each of us is given his (her) own gift" (Eph. 4:6–7, MSG).

Your gifts are the self-responsibilities given to you when you became an adult. Paul emphasized this in the same letter:

No prolonged infancies among us, please. We'll not tolerate babes in the woods, small children who are an easy mark for imposters. God wants us to grow up, to know the whole truth and tell it in love—like Christ in everything we do. He keeps us in step with each other. His very breath and blood flow through us so that we will grow up healthy in God, robust in love. (Ephesians 4:14–16, MSG)

You're most likely reading this book because your life feels out of control, helpless, meaningless, or dead-ended. The good news is your decision is taking positive steps toward spiritual, mental, emotional, and physical wellness. Spiritual guidance is connected to ethical decisions derived through spiritual discernment. Guidance and discernment begin the discovery of your capabilities to experience an awakening of your self-worth. You start off affirming your skills to act in healthy and productive ways. Listening to the voice and encouragement of God's Spirit mobilizes you to make wise and informed choices to become spiritually mature. You no longer are a victim of self-demise or helplessness. According to Paul, God's daily presence empowers your well-being "so you will grow up healthy in God, robust in love" (Eph. 4:14–15, MSG).

Discernment is being spiritually enlightened. Your mind and soul are intrinsically centered on receiving wise counsel through prayer, sacred teachings, meditation, and contemplation. The difference between meditation and contemplation is that meditation is a human mode of prayer, whereas contemplation is divinely inspired prayer. Meditation is a silencing of the clutter and clatter of your daily life. Meditation prepares you for contemplation, which is listening to the whispers of God. It's often called "Holy Listening" or "listening to the sacred."

Holy listening isn't about discovering your self-identity or self-confidence. It's about paying attention to God's presence and voice within and around you. Most of your past has been consumed listening to your voice or others. Discerning is purposeful listening to the holy and sacred word of God. Sometimes, it's simply listening to God with your heart, which isn't silence.

Leave your daily "busyness" and find a solitary place without distractions. Let your heart, mind, and soul be cleared yet open to an intimate encounter with God's Spirit. Instead of being self-centered and obsessed with your problems, feel the blessings of time spent in God's holy presence. It's not straightforward. It takes focused attention and time commitment. God is patiently waiting. Only you can begin this new adventure.

Seven

STEP FOUR: ACTUALIZING YOURSELF

*We acknowledge our self-defeating behaviors and seek God's wisdom
in becoming the self-actualizing persons we are created to be.*

In my late forties, I became somewhat overweight. My wife and I decided to challenge ourselves with a popular diet called "Fit for Life." Together, we changed our eating habits, often obsessing about the steps this diet required. We were excited when our weight and physical health improved. I became enamored with weight loss and a correlating increase in physical energy. I lost more weight than needed.

One day, while walking down the hall of our hospital, I heard one of the nurses from a distance say: "Stop it!"

"Stop what?" I replied. She was concerned that I was over adapting to my diet and that I needed to cease losing weight. She, like others, was curious about why I continued my current eating habits since I had reached my target weight and waist size. "You're not going to keep eating this way?" others asked. I said, "Yes!" I knew I hadn't set healthy limits and boundaries regarding this diet. Beware of obsessing or overadapting to any eating habits or spiritual guidelines for health.

My observation regarding unhealthy behaviors and habits is the constant denial of what changes require. Often, we convince ourselves that we can't change or that it's too difficult to accomplish. A fundamental, undeniable reality regarding physical health and spiritual well-being is that change only happens when you stop sabotaging yourself. One can't practice unhealthy living patterns and expect wellness. Once you quit undermining wise, healthy choices, your body, mind, and soul naturally move toward health.

God created us to be healthy beings. Health is within each of us. We continually violate the natural laws of health, believing we can escape the inevitable consequences. How deluded can one be?

The same spiritual laws apply to the well-being of your soul. Wholeness (salvation) is the inspirational process of becoming a whole person through God's Spirit. You're free to be responsive to the healing movement of God's presence and live fully (wholly) as God's creation. This freedom of choice means accepting responsibility for how you live. You can't determine the natural and spiritual laws or their outcomes. You've got the power to respond.

Examine your self-defeating behaviors if you genuinely desire to be physically, emotionally, socially, and spiritually healthy. There's no mystery to living in wellness. No secret diet, therapy, prescription, or religious practice allows you to ignore health principles and live wholesomely.

Stop whatever you're doing and believe in something that interrupts God's innate gift of a whole and healthy life. Living disgracefully means practicing the same old habits, denying God's source of well-being. Grace-filled living affirms, celebrates, and practices the natural and spiritual laws of wholeness.

You may be expecting a step-by-step guide for this miraculous change. What you need and may not know is that the consequence of change requires an open mind and your soul willing to explore the unknown, including the mysterious. You confront and face the consequences of poor choices from past to present. There's a difference between "disgrace" and "God-filled grace."

The origin of the word disgrace began in the 1580s and is rooted in French society of "honor" and "reproach." To deprive anyone of favor or good repute indicated treating them with disfavor. The scandal disgraced an individual or family with the consequences of shame and outcast. Disgrace is rooted in shame and a negative self-image. Saint Paul writes, "But we rejoice in our sufferings, knowing that suffering produces endurance, and endurance produces character, character produces hope. Hope does not put us to shame because God's love has been poured into our hearts through the Holy Spirit, who has been given to us" (Rom. 5:3–4, NIV).

Shame is a feeling. *Disgrace* is a noun disclosing your attitude and actions. There's a parallel between disgrace and dysfunction. Disgrace isn't a passive process. It's shame-based, as Paul explains. Interpersonal relations, from family to casual relationships, have impacted your past. One's self-concept is tarnished or stained with repetitive reinforcements by how others perceive you.

Coping with shame and disgrace is a spiritual challenge. It requires mental and emotional balance. You must discover and recover from blocked and locked perceptions of your life. It would be best to have faith to take a giant leap from the negativity overwhelming you. You're trapped in self-sabotaging, fear, anxiety, depression, distorted reality, agitation, irritation, and other defeating thoughts and actions. Breaking free from your bondage to unhealthy outcomes is possible and essential to your ultimate well-being. You begin with an attitude, emotional, and spiritual adjustment. Taking a vague inventory can be disturbing and frightening.

Self-sabotage is any activity or attitude preventing or interrupting your positive intent. In psychology, this is defined as cognitive dissonance. Human nature seeks consistent or constant results. We seek our actions, beliefs, and values to be in sync. When they aren't, our life feels out of control. You experience a sense of powerlessness, which is unacceptable. You feel your world is like a tropical storm or volcanic eruption. Your flawed being senses few options: give in to depression, isolation, suicidal thoughts, deprivation, mental and spiritual exhaustion, and so forth. How do you defeat self-sabotage?

Stop! An old saying suggests that if you want to dig a new hole, you don't dig the same hole deeper! Western comedian Will Rogers has been given credit for saying, "If you find yourself in a hole, the first thing to do is stop diggin'." It would be best if you adopted a different reality: new beginnings require stopping old beliefs, failed behaviors, distorted views, and spiritual lies. One of the more disturbing passages of the Gospel is spoken by Jesus:

If your right eye causes you to sin, gouge it out and throw it away. It is better for you to lose one part of your body than for your whole body to be thrown into hell. And if your right hand causes you to sin, cut it off and throw it away. It is better for you to lose one part of your body than for your whole body to go into hell. (Matt. 5:29–30, NIV)

What's Jesus claiming? He isn't referring to some ancient, barbaric ritual. No. He is speaking about adultery. However, he focuses on abusive behavior or harmful treatment of others and oneself. He uses an allegory or metaphor to instruct the disciples that lust is more than lust in one's heart. It's an action that violates the well-being of someone, including yourself. The intention of your mind and heart is vital to personal health and loving relationships. You could have an "intention deficit disorder." It resembles "attention deficit disorder," indicating a lack of healthy focus.

In a sermon, Leonard Sweet, author, and preacher, commented, "When Jesus said, 'If your eye or hand offend you, cut it off,' it was a vivid, symbolic way of saying that we must end doing those things that harm us and others. STOP is 'cutting out,' not 'cutting off.' The metaphor Jesus uses shows how serious it is to violate oneself and others."[21]

Once you dare to halt unhealthy thoughts and habits, you will experience a vacuum. Aristotle famously wrote about *horror vacui*, the principle commonly translated as "nature abhors a vacuum." New awareness and self-affirmation aren't immediate discoveries or experiences. In David's Song (Psalm 23), he alerts us to the periods and moments we walk through "the valley of death." It will seem like a dark and scary place. Death always precedes resurrection! No one desires to be in a "vacuum." It's because all life seeks a sense of wholeness, purpose, and meaning in the dimension of God's creation. But creation was born first out of the darkness before the light. There couldn't have been a "dawning" without the "darkness."

The well-known research scientist Stephen Hawking claimed, "If you feel you are in a black hole, don't give up. There's a way out."[22] Psalm 119:18 (ESV) declares: "Open my eyes that I may behold wondrous things out of your law." You've got an inner eye that can see the outer truth of God's Word. Hawking affirms the certainty of the Psalmist. You may sense living in a black hole, but God reveals there's a way out. Open your spiritual eyes to the incredible possibilities in your life.

Mind Tools teaches methods to overcome self-sabotage that deliberately destroys, damages, or prevents one from being successful or experiencing self-worth."[23] Self-sabotage is naturally self-limiting. It's undermining your best interest or reinforcing your negative self-image. It's a false effort to convince yourself, "I am of little value," or "I am a victim of how people treat me." It's exhibited in different ways: binge eating, drug abuse, hostile feelings, being supercritical, condescending, and avoiding coping with the problems or conflicts in your daily routines.

How's your unwell life capable of becoming in good health? You need an attitude adjustment. Attitude comprises your emotional, mental, and spiritual perceptions about your life. Your attitude is the internal stance taken toward the outward happenings in your life. Attitude is crucial to coping effectively with life's ups and downs.

If you've had trauma or are experiencing it, your fears can be overwhelming, and you feel unsafe. You may believe you don't deserve a new life. It's your inner voice trying to undermine good possibilities. Your catastrophic attitude lives daily with the expectation that only the worst will happen. While one may not want disappointments and feel defeated, this negative attitude does prepare you for the down times and seldom surprises. This expectation always keeps you tense and fearful. It seems normal.

What's the option? It's a faith perspective. It's an anastrophic (turning back) attitude that anticipates the best of things. This spiritual perception trusts in a positive journey. You believe and accept that God loves and affirms you. You move toward the possible, the hopeful, and the yet-to-be with faith and excitement. A faith stance helps you journey each day with serenity and enchantment. God's Spirit is the power and source of your capabilities and spiritual guide in this new adventure.

Your new or renewed faith perspective anticipates the arrival of each moment as a birthing of God's gift of life. This attitude doesn't ignore failure, pain, frustration, or downbeat endings. You'll know how to appropriate these experiences when they happen and not be destroyed by them. Discovering the "good" that seems present even amid what is "bad" or agonizing is possible.

You're getting ready for the joy and fulfillment of your hopes and dreams as a child of God. You've learned not to get trapped by resignation, cynicism, despair, or futility. The faith perspective is an investment, and trust in the promise of God's future is realized now. And this is breathtaking every time it happens.

Seeking God's wisdom is being an actualizing person. Accepting God's wise counsel gives you strength and trust in making sound decisions. It includes the principle of "grounding." Grounding is a way of discovering and experiencing God's truth. You discover truth through seeking God's wisdom.

Scripture says, "That you, being rooted and grounded in love, may have strength to comprehend with all the saints what is the breadth and length and height and depth, and to know the love of Christ that surpasses knowledge" (Eph. 3:17–19, ESV). Godly wisdom often requires doing that which is opposite your natural feelings or beliefs. It goes against the "conventional wisdom" of the day; it's not focused on self-preservation but sacrificing your needs for the sake of others. You can only live in godly wisdom and love in the Spirit (Gal. 2:20; Eph. 5:16, 25, ESV).

You can develop Godly wisdom by carefully selecting family and friends to journey through life with you: "Whoever walks with the wise becomes wise, but the companion of fools will suffer harm" (Prov. 13:20, ESV). You need God for strength in every windstorm. You want caring companionship for support. Be suspicious of "friends" who want to save your soul.

Be cautious of preachers who are more interested in the profits of their message than prophets of God's truth. Matthew's Gospel cautions, "Beware of false prophets, who come to you in sheep's clothing but inwardly are ravenous wolves" (Matt. 7:15, ESV).

Dr. Eugene Peterson's modern Bible translation is fresh: "Be wary of false preachers who smile a lot, dripping with practiced sincerity. Chances are they are out to rip you off some way or other. Don't be impressed with charisma; look for character" (Matthew 7:15, MSG).

What's keeping you grounded? Common terms need to be focused on the present. Being strong in your sense of self-worth. Having a sense of purpose. Deeply trust yourself in God's Spirit. Practice critical thinking (total attention) as described: "Don't look for shortcuts to God. The market is flooded with surefire, easygoing formulas for a successful life that can be practiced in your spare time. Don't fall for that stuff, even though crowds of people do.

The way to life—to God!—is vigorous and requires total attention" (Matt. 7:13–14, MSG).

Critical thinking has been expressed in many ways, but researchers generally agree that critical thinking involves rational, purposeful, and goal-directed thinking. This process guides you in making healthy decisions and choices in connection with spiritual thinking. It certainly corrects your self-defeating patterns of thinking and behaving. You're on the proper path of actualizing the person God created you to be.

Don't be gullible or naive when choosing your beliefs, attitudes, values, and relationships. God has given you a mind, soul, and heart. Learn to engage and interact with each one. It's a major example of asserting your self-actualizing ability.

According to psychologist Carl Rogers, human beings have an innate drive to grow as individuals and to achieve their full potential. He referred to this desire as the actualizing tendency. It is synonymous with the principle of "tropism," as mentioned in the previous chapter. Typically, tropism relates to biological organisms and their movement toward light or water sources to stay alive. But poets, philosophers, and theologians have used this term as a metaphor for renewed life.

Saint Luke emphasizes the teaching of Jesus: "Consider how the wildflowers grow. They do not labor or spin. Yet I tell you, not even Solomon in all his splendor, was dressed like one of these. If that is how God clothes the grass of the field, which is here today, and tomorrow is thrown into the fire, how much more will he clothe you—you of little faith" (Luke 12:27–28, NIV).

Unlike plants, your reactions happen only as you respond to God's actualizing power. It's not a simple or pain-free process. You were birthed distinctively special, as is all of God's creation. Every day you awaken, you face decisions and choices requiring spiritual clarity and a pure heart. Remain challenged with a strong purpose and a calling to follow the guidance of God's Spirit.

Former First Lady Michelle Obama is filled with compassion and wisdom. In her book *Becoming,* she wrote, "Becoming isn't about arriving somewhere or achieving a certain aim. I see it instead as forward motion, a means of evolving, a way to reach continuously toward a better self. The journey doesn't end."[24] She's a sensible and caring mentor to many people of all ages.

You'll have battles the longer you live, but never let them be a reason to quit living. Let your soul and heart walk in faith. It's not about life always being good but feeling good when life isn't! Reading this book will guide you to healthy options and spiritual inspiration for discovering pathways to a new life. There are many more important steps ahead that'll be valuable and rewarding.

Eight

STEP FIVE: HEALING ONE'S BROKENNESS

We will make a sincere spiritual audit of our lives and accept
God's grace-filled power to heal our inner brokenness.

I've had only one audit in my life. The IRS audited the nonprofit organization I owned. When I got notice of the pending audit, naturally, I was concerned and anxious. The auditor spent two days reviewing the financial records. Finally, he reported that all documents were accurate and that the audit was complete. What a relief! The emotions and discomfort of the process lingered for some time. I've heard, "An auditor is someone who tries to solve a problem you didn't know you had and in a way you don't understand." That's my sentiment!

An audit's value and purpose are carefully assessing the data's accuracy and verification in the business and financial realm. Regarding a spiritual audit, this is your responsibility and requires as much due diligence as any audit. God's Spirit guides this process, but you must pass a self-assessment to be the auditor.

You may be wondering how you hear the voice of God's Spirit. Mistakenly, you may expect a concrete voice to awaken you from your "slumbering" life. Longing to know what God expects of you or wanting a clear understanding of who you were born to be is an instinct. You can only hear God's silence when you cease listening to all the "noise" and voices of your outer world. Wonderfully, you're created with an inner voice that can commune with God's silent, whispering voice. Rumi, a thirteenth-century Persian poet, is world-renowned. He often wrote about the "soul quest":

> I looked in temples, churches, & mosques.
> But I found the Divine within my heart.
> There is a divine voice within us.
> That speaks only when
> Other voices are silent.
> Only in the silence
> His message is delivered.[25]

No one can see or hear anything with clarity in this world of confusion, babbling, and deceptive voices. Locating a place to experience silence or inner peace is a rarity. "Be still, and know that I am God," says Psalm 46:10 (KJV). Through all generations, stopping one's rambling and ill-focused life is evidence of your physical and spiritual sickness. Discover that inwardly there's a stillness and a sanctuary that will comfort you.

The invitation to audit or inventory your life requires silencing any outer voices and influences that can keep you in a box. The temptation to avoid or escape this inner quest is usual. However, you have a "critical inner voice" with a history of molding your "outer" self. It's where you start your Spiritual Inventory or audit.

Examining your heart and soul is an ancient tradition. As a boy, David prayed before being anointed as a king: "Search me, God, and know my heart; test me and know my anxious thoughts. See if there is any offensive way in me and lead me in the way everlasting" (Ps. 139:23–2, NIV).

David asked God to inventory his strengths and character to be a king. The inventory you'll be completing isn't about some calling from God. The focus and direction in which you're moving are a holistic understanding of every aspect of your life. It's guiding you through discovering "spiritual health," which transforms you mentally, socially, spiritually, and physically. The intent isn't about God's Spirit testing you. Instead, it's the self-examination of your life as God's gift of your birthing. Saint Augustine asserts, "God provides the wind, but man must raise the sails."

How pleased are you with the person you have become? What do you want that enhances your relationships with family, friends, and associates? Considering God's Spirit knows who and what you are, your task is to assess yourself about spiritual health or wholeness, in contrast to how others would describe you.

Let's begin with your mental and emotional attitude. They affect how you think, feel, and act. They influence or reflect on your psychological, physical, social, and spiritual well-being. You're a complex system, and it requires attentive and effective care. Your physical condition reveals all the symptoms related to the other systemic conditions. You've ignored the messages your body is telling. Headaches, stomach pains, nervous twitches, blurring eyes, and so forth speak to your inner voice and spiritual awareness. You seem to be living in an open tomb of your making.

You've read in previous chapters about being limited by negative self-talk, self-defeating behaviors, distorted perceptions, and stubbornness toward changing your life. These are the ingredients of what is called a "life map." A life map is a visual representation of all the significant moments in time that have shaped who you are, regardless of whether they were happy or sad occasions. Every day from birth until now, you create a life map bundled into reality. *Your* reality!

There's a distinction between mental illness and mental distortions. If you've been diagnosed with a mental disorder or are uncertain, stop reading and seek a therapist, psychologist, or psychiatrist as soon as possible. You can always return to reading books or publications to help you discover spiritual health.

Continuing with this current soul quest, you're learning and practicing how to balance mind, soul, spirit, and body in healthy, realistic steps that stir your natural healing powers. God's Spirit opens your soul and heart to a new life, a fresh beginning. But new beginnings won't evolve without ending, releasing, and letting go of all the baggage, making you a casualty of your oppression. You may be a mental and emotional victim of oppressive teachings or legalistic beliefs that have blinded or exploited you from freely responding to God's Spirit.

Paul said, "It is for freedom that Christ has set us free. Stand firm, then, and do not let yourselves be burdened again by a yoke of slavery" (Gal. 5:1, NIV); he's speaking about the freedom of conscience. No one should give away their power or let others control them.

Caring for yourself is a fundamental need and mission. Examine your beliefs, habits, and feelings to recognize mistaken or deceptive patterns. It's part and parcel of the life map you have been traveling on. Getting off that fruitless "treadmill" entails your journey ending here and now.

Be prepared to confront the facts affecting your mental and emotional condition. Become free from the forces of self-enslavement. You're the primary source of the mental and emotional restraints. Only you can free yourself from these self-controls. Come face-to-face with your puppet (ego) who blames and emotionally finds fault with your self-identity. You've taken on the mask of self-doubt and self-hatred and developed a belief system that accentuates your worthlessness, failure, inadequacy, and incompetence.

Or your life map has taken you down a different path that has consumed you with self-absorption, obsessive, controlling behavior, and persecution of others. Your "bully" nature forces ruler actions toward others. And others experience you as their tormentor. Your heart and soul lack sensitivity and compassion. There's darkness and emptiness surrounding your very being. People have become objects to control and material things to complete you.

Breaking free or giving up control can be strange and fearful. Genuinely being open to venturing on a radically new path means awakening your whole being to God's Spirit (Sacred Other). It's moments when you recognize and affirm that your deep desire and hope is to *live* your life!

Awakening is listening to your healthy inner voice (not inner critical voice or self-talk). It's both mental and spiritual in function. It's more than "intuition" yet included, but intuition and inner voice are connected. Awakening focuses on observing and practicing new realities or truths. You risk new possibilities and question every dimension of life: mental, emotional, social, spiritual, and physical. It's the reason for completing a Spiritual Inventory. You'll examine many issues related to becoming spiritually whole.

Historically, *awakening* has been called enlightenment, bliss, or nirvana. Famed psychiatrist Carl Jung made the idea of the spiritual awakening popular in the Western world. He described the process as returning to the original or natural Self. He believed the experience of rising to a higher state of consciousness has always been an intrinsic part of what it means to be human.

This conversion happens when your inner voice links with your inner vision. You begin seeing and listening to your world with new perspectives. It demands courage and integrity to expose lies, deceptions, destructive habits, and past immoral or abusive actions. It isn't a quick process. "Patience is the art of hope" was painted on a memorial. An awakening inspires hope and promises freedom from your old self.

Rebirth goes through a similar gestation to a natural birth. Relax and remain calm as your transformation evolves. It took years for your life map to be exposed. Now, you have the remainder of your life to reach the blessings of this new adventure. Don't fall into another trap of using self-assessment to reinforce old unhealthy thoughts and behaviors. Accept your past; be forgiving. Be thankful that you've committed to rebirth and renewal. Your trials and tribulations have taught you valuable lessons. Paul accepted his painful past as a blessing. He sent a message to the Church in Rome: "We rejoice in our sufferings, knowing that suffering produces endurance, and endurance produces character, and character produces hope" (Rom. 5:3–4, ESV).

Hope happens when you have the courage to accept what you can't change. Your past may contain memories of emotional and physical pain. The wounds have left unforgettable scars. You want to distance yourself from the agony and anger of such remembrances. You feel powerless and helpless when recalling such experiences. Nothing can change this truth. In Isaiah 43:25 (ESV), God says, "I, I am he who blots out your transgressions for my own sake, and I will not remember your sins."

How does your mental state enhance or harm your emotional status? If you're ashamed and guilty, your mind may have thoughts of self-harm or neglect. It's a way to punish those distorted feelings. When doing your Spiritual Inventory, remember these kinds of transactions. Your mental and emotional conflicts will naturally collide with social relationships. When your life seems to be in turmoil, your self-concept is reinforced or challenged. A healthy relationship involves openness, honesty, loving support, and trust. Everyone with an investment can be traumatized or estranged, whether this is a friend, significant other, family, or coworker.

God, the Creator, breathed life into Adam, and Eve was born of his flesh because of their basic need for a relationship. God is a relational Being. When you feel alienated, lonely, and unlovable, your heart, mind, soul, and spirit are most vulnerable. Your mind is warped, your feelings are without rhythm, your soul is in darkness, and your spirit has crashed. Will your Spiritual Inventory reveal a different picture?

Your body is equally affected in response to your unhealthy systems. In medical circles, stress is linked to harmful physical conditions such as high blood pressure, increased heart rate, and high blood sugar levels, and mental health issues such as anger, depression, and anxiety. Managing stress is a critical life skill that becomes essential over time. Your physical aches, sleepless nights, pounding heart, and grumbling stomach are relentless reminders of daily stress.

Ultimately, you're in mental despair, emotional spasms, spiritual apathy, and physical numbness. The common response to your imperfect life is over-reacting to those closest to you. I also believe that every relationship needs to be caring and affirming for the sanity and wellness of life.

The focus here is to acknowledge how your bodily health is bound to the mental, emotional, physical, and spiritual areas of one's life. You'll discover that what matters most is recognizing and accepting what is not working in your life. You'll find the keys to wellness that can bring inner calmness, balance, energy, and genuine joy about today and the many tomorrows to come. *Remember patience!*

Now attention shifts to the second part of Step Five: accept God's grace-filled power to heal our inner brokenness. Times of brokenness are moments when we feel most vulnerable and spiritually tender: "The Lord is close to the brokenhearted and saves the crushed in spirit" (Ps. 34:18, NIV). God's Spirit is present in those moments to reveal the strength beyond our strength. God's whispering gives comfort and strength to face whatever "brokenness" holds you captive.

In the fractured state, you feel helpless, abandoned, unworthy, and betrayed, with no options to escape this tormenting life. James 1:2–4 (ESV) says to "count it all joy, my brothers (sisters), when you meet trials of various kinds, for you know that the testing of your faith produces steadfastness. And let steadfastness have its full effect, that you may be perfect and complete, lacking in nothing."

There's a famous tradition in Japanese art called *Kintsugi*, meaning "golden joinery." It's the art of repairing something broken with gold, believing that the object is more attractive because it's broken. When a ceramic piece breaks, the masters of kintsugi repair it with gold, leaving the renewal highly visible because a recreated piece symbolizes fragility and tenderness for them.[26]

God's Spirit is such an artist. Taking your brokenness and repairing it like a precious gem creates a renewed human being. Your brokenness is accepted; it becomes a precious memory carried for the rest of your life. No one has been promised a life without pain. At times, you may feel like you are "falling apart." Losing a loved one, a friend, or a pet can be traumatic. Unresolved grief can entrap you in darkness. You may obsess about death—yours and others'. God promises you grace to bring healing. The loving God "heals the heartbroken and binds up their wounds" (Ps. 147:3, NIV). You've had your struggles, the pain, the wounds, and the traumas that have shaped your identity. You attempt to hide behind this shadowy deception, building a barrier between yourself and others.

Through spiritual awakening, God's grace invades your heart and soul. Like the man born blind who encounters Christ, the Sacred One, he's touched. Suddenly, his physical handicap and social shame are converted. His inner vision opens; his eyes sparkle with beauty and hope. He's healed from the lifelong darkness and can dance like a butterfly. He's free from the catacomb. The chrysalis has happened. He can become one of the Easter people. The delightful poet Maya Angelou said it another way: "Become a rainbow in someone else's clouds."[27]

Don't let your mind and soul submit to disturbing or unwanted thoughts. If you attempt to control these responses, you'll immediately feel anxious; your stomach (body) tightens up, and cramps set in. Your body is the vessel housing thoughts and emotions. Chemistry and biology impact our moods, emotions, thoughts, and beliefs. These synergistic feedbacks are vital messages to your entire self that you're sick and need help. Avoiding or denying their notices only compounds the problem. When any parts of your senses are out of sync, pay attention.

Your soul asks what the mind seeks, how the spirit inspires and encourages health, and how the body manages it. The proper link between the four is imperative to a healthy lifestyle. The Scripture affirms a strong connection between physical, emotional, and spiritual health. For example, it is written, "A cheerful heart is good medicine, but a crushed spirit dries up the bones" (Prov. 17:22, NIV).

In what way does God's (Divine Spirit) grace bring wholeness or healing? Grace is Spirit-centered. Grace is a gift of God. You don't earn it, deserve it, or control it. In our Western culture, we pride ourselves on creativity, self-will, and problem-solving. We shape our future. We got ourselves into this human situation. We abide by the Marine cadence: "Stand up, buckle up, shuffle to the door, Jump right out and shout MARINE CORPS! If that one should fail me too, look out devil, I'm a-comin' for you!"[28]

Grace doesn't work that way. Instead, it teaches us to let go and let God. Not only are you not in charge, but you also don't have to be. It would be best if you stayed open to receiving sacred healing. Your freedom allows you to accept or reject the gift of grace. Receiving grace-filled healing means you're bursting with humility and profound gratitude. Since grace is unconditional love, we are then to love unconditionally. God's love is unconditional and uncontrolling. Love isn't manipulative or controlling. If this is true, then we must live by the same conditions. You can't assume you have powers; not even God (Spirit) has. Grace is grace and not penance.

Let's explore the Spiritual Inventory. There are guidelines and suggestions to consider before starting this process. I encourage you to have a journal that is related to your current quest. A spiral notebook can keep the inventory centralized. This inventory will require finding a serene place without electronics. Silence (without noise) is free of any interference or interruptions. Go music-free, with the TV off and iPhone muted. Snacks with hydration are fine. Allow time for breaks but no diversions like answering or calling on your phone.

It's a holy and sacred means of hearing and seeing with your inner voice and vision. God's Spirit is present for nurturing and inspiring self-discovery.

There are seven venues to explore. Each venue has eight questions or statements. There's no timeline or order to follow. However, many questions are sequential, meaning one response may require an answer first. One suggestion is to complete a venue before another because once you concentrate on one, your train of thought needs to remain single-minded. Return to a venue when you desire to change or add comments.

A Spiritual Inventory

Venue One: Awareness of the Holy

1. What or who is sacred to you?
2. What are your feelings when thinking of God, Spirit, or Sacred Being? If none, why not?
3. What is most important in your life?
4. What is your first thought or reaction to spirituality?
5. Was there a time when God, Higher Power, or Creator became more than a name to you? When? How? If never, why?
6. In what ways have you experienced or sensed the awe and wonder of life?
7. What do you consider an absolute no or taboo for you? For others?
8. What is the most significant change of having God's Spirit or spiritual being in you? If none, why?

Venue Two: Sense of Meaning

1. What is your purpose in life? Are you doing it and enjoying fulfilling it?
2. What holds the most meaning for you in life?
3. What does the future hold for you?
4. What are your feelings regarding death?
5. Do you believe there is an afterlife? What do you think about it?
6. What would you do if you had one year to live?

7. What would it say if you could write your epitaph? What would others write?
8. What brings you the most satisfaction in life?

Venue Three: Sense of Belonging (Communion)

1. Do you belong to a particular group or organization? What is the reason you or don't?
2. Who are the people caring for you the most? Why?
3. Do you prefer being alone or with other people? Why?
4. Who do you genuinely care for and spend time with? Why?
5. Do you ever feel lonely? How do you cope with loneliness?
6. What are the characteristics you want in a friend?
7. Do you usually feel equal to the people you associate with?
8. Do you have close friends? Explain why or why not.

Venue Four: Sense of Grace and Forgiveness

1. Have you ever been upset because you said or did something to another person? How did you deal with it?
2. Have you ever committed a wrong toward another person? Did you acknowledge this to that person? Did you ask for forgiveness? How did you feel?
3. Has anyone asked you for forgiveness? If yes, how did you respond and feel? If not, why do you believe this hasn't happened?
4. Have you ever blamed someone for what happened or happened to you? Has anyone blamed you for what happened or happened to them? Do you blame yourself now for what happened to someone in your life? How have you dealt with it?
5. Is there anything you have done or not done for which you want forgiveness? Explain.
6. Do you feel God accepts you and you're forgiven? Explain.
7. How has God's grace been most evident in your life?
8. Do you enjoy your life and who you are? Explain.

Venue Five: Sense of Faith and Trust

1. What do you do that is risky? Explain your response.
2. What do you do for fun and relaxation?
3. Do you ever have doubts, and how do you deal with them? If you have none, then why not?
4. Is it essential for you to be right? Why or why not?
5. How do you respond to not knowing something?
6. Do you get what you want most of the time? If yes, why? If not, why?
7. What is the most challenging thing about trusting others? Or let others trust you? If it is not difficult, why is that?
8. How have you let God guide you in your life? Have you always gone where God's Spirit leads you? Why or why not?

Venue Six: Sense of Being Spiritually Whole

1. What characteristics do you have that remind you of God, Higher Power, or Creator? Explain.
2. Can others sense a spiritual presence in your life? Why or why not?
3. How would you describe yourself? How would others tell you? How would the Divine Spirit (God's Spirit) describe you?
4. Do you see the image of love and humility in others? In what way? If not, why?
5. Do you have difficulty being kind and affirming to others? Why?
6. In what way would you want to be different? Why?
7. What would it be if you could change one thing about yourself? Why?
8. Do you care for yourself physically, mentally, and soulfully? Explain.

Venue Seven: Sense of Ecstasy and Passion

1. What excites and thrills you? How frequently does this happen? Why or why not?
2. Do you have the energy to do what you want to? Why? How?
3. What do you do for renewal and spiritual nourishment?

4. How can you go about finding more passion in your life?
5. Do you like to dance and sing? Why or why not?
6. Do you tend to be rigid and want to be in control in relationships? Explain.
7. What could you do differently to have more joy and energy?
8. What can you do to stop sabotaging your spiritual growth? What pro-active measures can you take to experience spiritual wholeness?

Nine

Step Six: Leap of Faith

We take a leap of faith and disclose our inner selves to others to acknowledge God's acceptance and forgiveness of our lives.

A leap of faith, interestingly, isn't a phrase or term mentioned in the Bible. It comes from a translation of the Latin words *saltus fidei*. The Danish philosopher Søren Kierkegaard formed this phrase as a metaphor for religious belief in God. He argued that God was spiritual rather than physical and was separate from the material world, including humankind. I'm not a believer in this view of God. But I do have an appreciation for this slogan.

Faith is active and not passive. It's a dynamic process. It's beyond a casual walk down a path. It's a motivating sensation like saying, "I can feel it in my bones!" or "I can leap for joy!" There's no promise or guarantee of success. Faith reaches out to the unknown and is not captive to fear. The author of Hebrews understood: "Faith is the substance of things hoped for, the evidence of things not seen" (Heb. 11:1, KJV).

In this chaotic and confusing world, risking seems to defy the possibilities of a loving, kindly, and engaging life. The 1992 movie *Leap of Faith* stars Steve Martin as a religious con artist. In his words, and his role as Jonas Nightengale, he admits being a fake. He confesses to a young boy healed that night, "I had nothing to do with you walking." Take note of his leap of faith testimony: "Never underestimate the power of belief, boy." He confesses to witnessing people who believed in miracles, though he never performed one. What courage it takes to recognize and admit your character faults.[29]

Another movie, *The Michael Jackson Story*, featured the popular song "Man in the Mirror." It suggests self-reflection.[30] Spiritual health involves coming face-to-face, gazing at yourself in a mirror. A mirror is commonly used for inspecting oneself, such as personal grooming—thus the old-fashioned name "looking glass."

A mirror is a reflection revealing how you see yourself. Paul realized this: "For now we see in a mirror dimly, but then face to face; now I know in part, but then I will know fully just as I also have been fully known" (1 Cor. 13:12, ESV).

Step Six has the conditions to challenge and expand your life. You'll learn the dynamics of faith, disclosure, acceptance, and forgiveness. Initiating the sixth step indicates being open and ready to "leap" beyond your normal boundaries. You need the inner strength to leap across the chasm of your mind, soul, heart, and body. Your heart and soul are front and center as you accept the truth of who you are. You aren't prepared to disclose yourself to others until you recognize and accept your true self.

Leaping is surrendering to the not-yet. You can't demand a promised outcome. You aren't jumping into darkness; the unknown is filled with possibilities. It's unimaginable to discover the magical dimensions of a "brave new world." Give up wishful thoughts of wanting to change without disciplined action. It isn't a New Year's resolution repeated annually. An old saying suggests that "if you want to dig a new hole, you don't dig the same hole deeper!"

It should be obvious that getting out of your pit by continuing to live with the same habits, beliefs, and expectations is a dead end. You're called to surrender, which implies giving up whatever keeps you in bondage to self-destruction and demeaning relationships. You can't become who you want to be until you stop being who you are.

Leaping is giving up your controlling attitudes and behaviors. You're letting go, which liberates you to respond to God's Spirit spontaneously. The "God of your understanding" has a more excellent vision and purpose for your life: "If we live by the Spirit, let us also keep in step with the Spirit" (Gal. 5:25, ESV). A leaping faith trusts that a power and life force guides you. But you need to act. A young woman gave me her poem about sobriety at the close of her drug treatment, requesting anonymity. She discovered what it means to surrender:

> As children bring their toys to us,
> With tears for us to mend
> I brought my broken dreams to God
> Because he was my friend.
> But then, instead of leaving Him
> In peace to work alone
> I hung around and tried to help
> with ways of my own.
> At last, I snatched them back and cried,
> "How can you be so slow?"
> "My child," He said, "What could I do?
> "You never did let go!"

The leap-of-faith metaphor is more than a catchphrase. It's a meaningful way to explain how you can break free from habits and beliefs that have plagued you. Before taking chances with self-disclosure, you need first to risk accepting yourself. You may carry so much emotional and mental baggage that needs unpacking, and self-identity lacks clarity.

You may have lived under guilt, remorse, rejection, and stagnant feelings for some time, so there is little sense of what is real or false. You mask your identity. Some think of the words in Proverbs 4:23 (ESV): "Keep your heart with all vigilance, for from it flow the springs of life are a precaution for revealing yourself." However, your heart is the motivating factor in choosing to be freed from any pain, traumas, or agonizing loss.

If you carry this baggage, your uncomfortable feelings will darken your soul. Your soul becomes weary from carrying the burden. Why do you hesitate? Most likely, you've become familiar with the discomfort and have adapted and accepted a common comment: *it is what it is!*

Perhaps you've been fooled, believing you're unworthy. Considering all your past decisions, failures of trying, and feelings of being ignored or abused, the thought of venturing into an alien world is frightening! Why be disappointed again? The leap of faith is built on the foundation of hope. Here's a promise to remember: "And hope does not put us to shame, because God's love has been poured out into our hearts through the Holy Spirit, who has been given to us" (Rom. 5:5, NIV). God gives hope that supports us during times of disappointment. This kind of hope is found not in avoiding suffering but in working through it because suffering produces perseverance; perseverance, character; and character, hope.

Rather than living you merely exist in a living death. You can refuse to make the choices that let go of a "dead past." Instead of burying your wounds and grief, you celebrate them. Learn to dialogue with the memories and feelings of yesterday. A new day dawns when you accept the past; receive it with thankfulness and discover the strengths that have shaped you through all the trials.

As stated in Step Six, a leap of faith is the willingness to disclose your inner self to others. Self-disclosure is risky. It signifies "opening" your heart, exposing your feelings, and letting someone enter your circle of comfort. If you previously struggled with limits and boundaries in relationships, this step requires precautions and wise decisions when reaching out.

Boundaries are rules, limits, or guidelines someone sets to let others know what they are comfortable and uncomfortable with. Boundaries help you identify how far and how much you are willing to share, not knowing how other people behave toward them and what will happen if those boundaries are broken.

Selectivity and appropriateness of self-revelation understand the who, what, when, and where these conversations occur. Have an awareness of the person or situation with whom this will happen. Time and place are equally crucial when taking this leap of faith and sharing your heart, mind, soul, or beliefs.

Everyone needs to feel safe when self-disclosing. Healthy boundaries are the foundations of healthy relationships. It's the way individuals discover affirmation and self-respect. Love and appreciation sustain friendships, marriages, families, coworkers, first responders, schools, churches, and all residents who share this remarkable space we call home.

Spiritual wholeness is caring, serving, partnering, sacrificing, and committing to kind, loving, and forgiving relations. If you focus on your inadequacies or self-doubts, trusting others to accept your desire to share yourself or be vulnerable is limited. Establishing and trusting boundaries is the perfect environment for a relationship to evolve and grow.

Setting a boundary is important because it keeps your self-identity intact, and you avoid becoming entangled in an unhealthy relationship. *Enmeshment* is a psychological term describing a toxic relationship in which you depend on someone else for all your emotional needs. Or you maintain control of a relationship by agreeing to meet all the emotional needs of another. Both of you live in misery and loneliness.

You want to build a bridge, not a wall, relating to others. A bridge keeps the lanes open in both directions. A wall doesn't protect you—it only reinforces the distance between you. Openness and discretion are partners. Your willingness to be vulnerable allows you to share meaningful information without violating the boundaries of the one with whom you're sharing. Paul encouraged the church in Philippi to live a life of service and obedience. He encouraged people who are not afraid to give: "Do nothing from selfish ambition or conceit, but in humility count others more significant than yourselves. Let each of you look not only to his interests but also to the interests of others" (Phil. 2:3–4, NIV).

You may have spent most of your life figuring out the reasons for personal suffering, meaninglessness, emptiness, loneliness, and even worthlessness. This step focuses on how to stop comparing yourself to others. Discovering a healthy identity and becoming a loving and forgiving person of yourself and others.

God can't forgive or accept you until you have the strength and courage to accept yourself. You probably have difficulty accepting the harmful, mean things you said or did recently or in the past. You're trapped in guilt and remorse. Your life is likely filled with misconceptions and downright fabrications about God. Your mind, much less your spirit, can't believe or accept a description of God who suffers with you. It's God's ultimate way of holding us in the arms of compassion. Theologian Thomas Jay Oord maintains: "God is the fellow sufferer who understands. God is moved with compassion and affected by the ups and downs of our lives. God empathizes with us better than any friend could."[31]

Theologians and biblical scholars argue against this teaching because they hold that God isn't relational in any personal form. However, God's presence manifesting through Christ gives us a different portrait. "I and the Father are one," said Jesus (John 10:30, KJV).

Pay close attention to the phrase in Step Six: we "disclose...to others to acknowledge God's acceptance and forgiveness of our lives." When God forgives you, it's shown by how you relate to others. God's mercy isn't a momentary decision. It's for all your past, present, and future misdeeds. In 1 John 1:9 (NIV), we learn this: "But if we confess our sins to him, he is faithful and just to forgive us our sins and to cleanse us from all wickedness." However, be prudent: "Love prospers when a fault is forgiven, but dwelling on it separates close friends" (Prov. 17:9, ESV).

You may have lost an important relationship due to the failure of one or the other to forgive. Like you and all those connected to your life, you're flawed human beings, and eventually, you will run into misunderstandings even with those you love. You might unintentionally hurt others, as others may trouble you. When you forgive a failing, love is repaired. In turn, remain open to accepting the forgiveness of anyone who may have bruised your heart and soul.

The eighth step of Alcoholics Anonymous uses a more focused term when speaking about forgiveness: "Made a list of all persons we had harmed and became willing to make amends to them all."[32] The harm mentioned here is directly related to the life of an alcoholic or drug addict. While this may apply to you, Step Six in this book refers to all words and actions you've used (intentionally or accidentally) to harm others. You'll note that this issue is included in the Spiritual Inventory but doesn't indicate identifying those you have hurt by name.

Amends isn't about feeling sorry or guilty so that you can be free of emotional or spiritual pain. It's more than an apology or alleviating guilt. You're making things right with someone who needs forgiveness. Offering amends can have therapeutic benefits. You acknowledge God's acceptance and for-giveness when you act with a penitent heart. The broken relationship with God or Sacred Being is healed, and your heart and soul find strength and solace. Ultimately, you learn to be accountable by making amends and dis-covering your humanness. Perfection isn't possible. Fallibility is a character strength.

Probably, it'll take time to accept this reality. You may feel painful, un-comfortable, or uncertain, but you'll sense the power and amazement of this rebirth. You'll grow through new and unexpected experiences. Refreshing moments happen in your relationships with yourself and your capacity to love others.

Here's the caution: the ninth step of Alcoholics Anonymous alerts you when and when not to make amends: "Made direct amends to such peo-ple wherever possible, except when to do so would injure them or others."[33] While you may be prepared to make reconciliation, there's no guarantee that the proposed recipient(s) of your amends will be accepted.

Your changed heart and mind are acting with humility and kindness. You treat others, respecting the importance of their hearts and minds. Realize that not everyone is prepared or able to receive or return such forgiveness or amends. Their emotional and psychological health may be impaired, prevent-ing reasonable responses.

If you've been a victim of emotional, physical, or sexual abuse, consult someone who can advise you on the practical approach to this abuser. Prayer-fully consider the various options and plan how you will confront this situa-tion (in the future).

You're progressing in this spiritual quest and learning new skills in caring for yourself. Sometimes, making amends won't be enough to restore trust. Your need and desire to repair the relationship won't mean they are. Don't take any action that potentially can push you into the shadows from which you've been freed. If making amends will open old wounds or create new harm, then making direct amends should be avoided. Your future will eventu-ally equip you with the skills to confront these complicated issues.

It may be wise not to go down this path of making amends until you have completed all twelve steps of the soul quest. Accepting yourself is a major achievement, and lovingly nurturing yourself through forgiveness is God's gift of grace. Focus on less troublesome relationships, the ones you may experience joint returns.

You're building the foundation and framework for a spiritually whole and healthy life. The adventure of your soul quest opens new and exciting ways to reclaim self-identity and self-worth. At the core of spiritual health is the force of healing. Note that the word "heal" precedes "thy"; "thy will be done" is the guiding principle of the Lord's Prayer.

God's Spirit embraces your body, filling you with warmth and calming your heart with serenity. The Spirit's awesome presence holds you with tenderness and energizes your spirit to grasp hold of the impossible and unbelievable. You're alive; each breath you breathe is a reminder of the goodness of God and the sacredness bestowed on you and others humbled by this voyage called *life*! You're honored to share in the grandeur of God's creation. You're cherished as one of the caretakers of this great wonder.

Never minimize your value considering the importance of what God has in store for you and the purpose for which you're born. Stop discounting yourself, feeling useless, sensing no life intention, and merely existing in the doldrums! Escape the monotonous routines you experience daily whirling around in a squirrel cage. At least a squirrel has enough common sense to search for acorns and play tag around an oak tree with his friends.

We'll explore your purpose and challenge you to achieve a meaningful and enjoyable life. You'll uncover an abundance of joy when you accept and grant forgiveness. Step Nine will unwrap that gift. Concentrate on Step Six, which is finding ways to forgive and make amends.

Another question when considering all the implications of this step: How do you know God accepts you? Are there any preconditions you need to consider? Generally, being kind and polite to others seems proper and natural. However, everyday observation sees how easily people can offend or be offended. You wonder what are "proper" or "correct" attitudes and behaviors to avoid hurting anyone's feelings? Christ faced this problem frequently. His disciples constantly questioned his parables (metaphors) and were annoyed by how he accepted the most blatant "sinner." He had a different standard of relating to seemingly "outcasts" and invalids. He even touched the untouchables who were plagued with leprosy.

Are you ready and willing to care for those who aren't your equal? Can you invite the homeless street "bums" to your home? Are you capable of sacrificing your needs to hold in your arms the sick and suicidal? God's Son showed us how to love and care for others, not just those most like us. This invitation is to everyone whom God loves and accepts. That's everybody!

Come to me, all you who are weary and burdened, and I will give you rest. Take
my yoke upon you and learn from me, for I am gentle and humble in heart, and
you will find rest for your souls. For my yoke is easy and my burden is light.
—Matthew 11:28–3, NIV

God's mission through the sacrificial Son was to reveal the authentic character and practice of being a child in a promised land who's welcomed into the household of faith through grace. This household of faith isn't the Temple, the Church, or organized religion. It's the sacred fellowship of the human family. It's the birthright of all humanity. We're connected to all religious traditions and fellowship as kindred souls. Broaden your image of who's included in your list of ones needing forgiveness and amends.

Ten

STEP SEVEN: BUILDING, SHARING, AND CARING SUPPORT

*We claim in humility our God-given gifts, and we will joyfully share who
and what we are as we build caring support for ourselves and others.*

One of the greatest love stories in all mythical literature is about Narcissus and Echo. Narcissus was forecasted, as a child, that he would live a long life only if he "never discovered himself." As he grew older, Narcissus relished walking through the woods. One day, Echo, a mountain nymph, saw him and fell deeply in love. So she watched him from a distance, but not enough, because Narcissus suspected he was being followed. He stopped and yelled, "Who's there?" Echo repeated, "Who's there?"

Narcissus, startled, quickly moved away and told Echo to leave him alone. She became bewildered and distraught. Yet she searched daily in the remote woods, never seeing or hearing Narcissus again. Nothing was left, only her echo.

Nemesis, the goddess of revenge, decided to punish Narcissus after hearing the story of Echo. Nemesis enticed Narcissus to a pond during a summer hunting trip to satisfy his thirst. Gazing into the mirroring water, he saw the face of a handsome youth.

He did not recognize his reflection and fell in love with this magical image. Unable to separate himself from the carbon copy, Narcissus never experienced mutual love. It's said that "he melted away from the fire of passion burning inside him, eventually turning into a gold and white flower."[34] This century is an age of narcissism, as evident in social media. We're becoming corrupted by our senses of self, which reshapes us into grandiose, self-infatuated image-makers. Narcissism is a belief that some people have "entitled self-importance." These are people who think they're special and deserve special treatment.

As a society, way too many are self-invested and have self-indulgent attitudes. The time has come for us to break this cycle of a socially diseased nation. The ultimate objective of Step Seven is discovering and creating communities, partnerships, companionships, and faith fellowships.

Usually, there's an imbalance of people who are victims of self-destruction and others who want to destroy those who are different or not like themselves. Too many feel disenfranchised, sensing they're "strangers in a foreign land." *This is not my home* is their cry. Sadly, those who feel unloved, incapable of love, doubt they will ever find love. The reality of life can be disturbing to those who concentrate on the anguish and misguided views of pessimists, the distorted beliefs of the deranged, and the hostility of hate-mongers, all victims of their demented assumptions about our human existence.

I assume you're reading this book to uncover or recover the healthy options you can adopt for character strength. You're discovering the rewarding potential and possibilities of a refreshing and renewed life. Remember, you must be intentional and committed to applying the lessons guiding you in following these twelve steps to spiritual wholeness. There's nothing simple or easy about your soul quest.

The opposite of self-obsession is *humility*. Selfishness is the infection of the soul. One's heart hardens if left untreated. Your spirit withers. Alone, without family or friends, your circle of relationships shrivels to ashes. Communities, friendships, companionships, and partnerships become illusions. Isolation becomes desolation.

There's no disgrace in affirming one's self-worth. What's destructive is self-exaggeration. Some mistakenly believe they are enough to satisfy and meet their own needs. Others either disregard or discount the importance of others. When "pride" treats others as subjects, it creates hostile and abusive interactions. C. S. Lewis observed this disaster. He wrote: "Pride leads to every other vice: it is the complete anti-God state of mind…it is Pride which has been the chief cause of misery in every nation and every family since the world began."[35]

Humility is the "freedom from pride or arrogance." Humility is a virtue, and it trumps pride. Paul urges the church in Philippi, "Do nothing from selfishness or empty conceit, but with humility of mind regard one another as more important than yourselves; do not merely look out for your own personal interests, but also for the interests of others" (Phil. 2:3–4 NIV).

The writer of Proverbs testifies, "When pride comes, then comes disgrace, but with humility comes wisdom" (11:2, NIV). How does wisdom grow from humility? God has blessed you with a humble heart and an open mind. God's Spirit uses these "*gifts*" to affirm the passion and love within you.

You long to fully know yourself. The soul quest channels your desire through wisdom and humility to realize this dream. Your mind is gaining the knowledge needed to tell the truth of your story. You dare to be honest about who and what you are. Self-emptying frees you from the burdens of the past. There will be times when this emptying process feels like a void. However, what you're experiencing is the most demanding part of this journey. God's Spirit can only fill your needs when you cease the need to be in control and acknowledge, "*I am drained.* I can't give to others what I don't have." Or, as Albert Einstein reasoned, "The more you know, the more humble you become." And this is the beginning of wisdom.

In my younger years, I spent many summers with my maternal grandparents. My grandmother was an excellent cook, especially pies. She surprised me one day with a new and different pie. The first taste startled my senses; it was tart, and I coughed it up. "It's rhubarb," she said. I rudely commented, "What's that?" She answered, "You better watch out, or I will feed you humble pie." She explained the moral of this tale: "If you can't say something nice, don't say anything!"

The phrase derives from *umble*, which refers to inner animal parts, the original name of the meat pie, considered inferior food. In medieval times, the pie was often served to lower-class people. But this understanding doesn't appreciate the blessings in a humble soul. Some believe humility is an innate quality within the soul and our ego develops in our natural growth, but someone with humility is simply in a state of self-respect. When we come from a place of inner self-respect, we feel secure, and humility can grow. Others suggest humility is learned and nurtured within a family, church, and caring relationships. If you grew up in an abusive environment, repeatedly treated with little or no self-value, you might feel defeated before you begin.

Aristotle understood humility as a moral virtue sandwiched between the vices of arrogance and moral weakness. I consider humility interconnected with wisdom. Humility makes you aware that you bring worth to this world and many others.

Humility includes attitude, which is a subject we discussed in chapter two. It's composed of your emotional and spiritual perceptions about life. Attitude is the internal stance toward the outward happenings in your life. Attitude is crucial to coping effectively with life's ups and downs.

People with a catastrophic attitude expect daily for only the worst to happen. While one may not want disappointments and to feel defeated, this negative attitude does prepare you for the down times, and you're seldom surprised by them. This expectation always keeps you tense and fearful.

The other option is to assume an anastrophic attitude that anticipates the best things. It's a spiritual perception that trusts in a positive journey. You move toward the possible, the hopeful, and the yet-to-be with faith and excitement. The faith stance helps you to journey each day with serenity and enchantment. Humility happens when you embrace this attitude. You look forward to the arrival of each moment as a birthing of God's gift of life. This attitude doesn't ignore failure, pain, frustration, or downbeat endings. But you do know how to accept these experiences when they happen and not be destroyed by them.

Discovering the "good" in what seems "bad" or agonizing is possible. It prepares you for the joy and fulfillment of hopes and dreams as God's child. It reminds you not to get trapped by resignation, cynicism, despair, or futility. The faith perspective invests and trusts in the promise of God's future, which is now. And this is exciting every time it happens. You're dancing with joy! Wisdom-filled humility develops the joyful sharing of your healthy self-identity and building caring support systems to sustain your progress. Coplanning and copartnering will bring many blessings.

Before exploring the importance of building a caring support system, let's reflect on the value of "joyful sharing." Joy is a relational dynamic. Joy has meaning only when shared. Joy is expressed in music, poetry, art, dancing, clapping, laughing, and warm embracing. Romans 15:13 (ESV) declares, "May the God of hope fill you with all joy and peace in believing, so that by the power of the Holy Spirit you may abound in hope."

Happiness tends to be momentary, an outward expression limited to a time and place, like attending a concert. On the other hand, joy is an inner experience of oneself and is remembered often. It's a genuine part of your history; you delight in sharing.

There's a charming story about a little girl who asked her mother, "How come whenever I open up a flower it falls apart, but when God opens it up it stays together?" The mother was puzzled by the question. Before she could reply, the child interrupted, saying, "Oh, I know. When I open it up, I open it from the outside, but when God opens it up, it is from the inside."

Joy happens first in one's heart before you seek to share it. Joy is sometimes the response to a healing soul. Grieving becomes a joy when mourning is at rest. King David understood this with all his trials and challenges. He was grateful to God, saying, "You have turned my mourning into dancing; you have loosed my sackcloth and clothed me with gladness" (Ps. 30:11, NIV).

Joy is so awesome that you may have difficulty sharing it. Your brain releases certain chemicals called dopamine and serotonin when you're excited. Usually, you feel flushed and a little lightheaded. Your heart beats faster, and you can't stop smiling or laughing. Don't worry; it's normal to feel contrasting physical sensations in reaction to your joyful emotions and to have different bodily responses than those around you.

Avoid the illusions of joy. There's no magical pill or perfect relationship. Beware of social media, where endless promises or products seduce you in scams to fulfill fantasies, daydreams, and cravings with minimal investment of self or money. Remember, joy is an internal process, and no outer bargain will satisfy the needs of your mind, heart, soul, and body.

At its core, Buddhism teaches the sacredness of life and a devotion to the creativity and novelty of daily living. It invites us to avoid the sameness in our ordinary life. Our daily life is often monotonous. To discover life's sacredness, you need a new set of lenses to enjoy everything with a fresh outlook. Every moment is full of aroma and zest.

Perhaps you're starting to understand how joy relates to building a caring support system. A caring community is vital in maintaining your well-being and that of others. The benefits of caring release oxytocin, a brain chemical sometimes called the "love hormone." It's associated with empathy, compassion, trust, intimacy, and the fostering of relationships.

Successful and rewarding relationships are formed. They don't surface without kind, loving, and trusting intent to risk the challenges of forming more caring and intimate relations. However, loving and caring aren't sufficient for forming lasting relationships. They require discipline, attention, and intention.

Let's examine some core principles of caring for yourself and others. They're essential to developing or engaging in meaningful relationships. I've been selective in my list. Some professionals have many criteria as fundamental principles. You may choose to expand the listing. These will at least open the door to healthy *resolutions*.

Bonding is called the "art of attachment." It's full of emotions such as affection and trust. It's considered social connection, the experience of feeling close and linked to others. It involves feeling loved, cared for, and valued, forming the basis of acceptance. Connection happens when two people sense being present, listened to, and appreciated. They feel nurtured, and their relationship strengthens. The absence or loss of bonding when growing up provokes low self-esteem, alienation, hostility, aggression, and antisocial behavior. Children in this model of a family either become victims of bullying or initiate such violent behavior.

The outcome for adults who fail to bond daily is physical and emotional abuse. Once again, they're either abusers or victims of abuse. It's common for these individuals to historically be members of family systems where this was the norm. Regrettably, this is the DNA of such families, and they believe this is common. It's known as "trauma bonding."

You can have valuable encounters without suffering abusive trauma. There are challenging and distressing experiences that can strengthen relationships. Bonding involves shared experiences. Bonds mature through difficult times, and you can learn how to support each other. Bonding is critical to your fulfillment and happiness. Understanding these can help you build, leverage, and maintain long-term bonds. Bonding includes connecting your positive and negative experiences.

You create an environment of belonging and enhance your emotional and spiritual well-being. You recognize how much your life in the past has known deep isolation and loneliness. In fact, the more complex the experience, the more bonding may occur. The good news is that you can look forward to more excellent connections and new levels of closeness when risking healthy bonding. Someone once said, "When we're together, everything falls into place."

I don't know the source, but I remember the insight: "We may not have it all together, but together we have it all." Scripture is more precise: "And above all these put on love, which binds everything together in perfect harmony" (Col. 3:14, ESV). Caring support systems have catalyzed a network of people who can provide practical or emotional support. They'll help you improve your overall health and reduce stress and anxiety. Having a support system means having people to rely on when you need them the most.

Another principle essential to caring relationships is *mutual respect*. Respect values who the other is and appreciates the other person's boundaries. You're courteous and kind, accepting each other's differences. Affirming individuality recognizes that no two people are alike. You won't always find an agreement or concur with collective decisions. However, your dignity and self-worth are never compromised or discounted. Love and continual support nurture you through these periods. Character increases, and emotional and spiritual healing is happening.

God created us for relationships; they shouldn't expect or demand that we violate our values or cease caring for ourselves. Don't sacrifice your hopes and dreams. No healthy, loving, or forgiving relationship can survive without a tenacious spirit and a heart willing to take risks. You haven't come this far to settle for less.

Mutual respect is setting limits on one's desires and living within those limits with satisfaction. Each relationship you seek has different expectations. It makes sense to be patient and selective in whatever relationships you form. You want to be comfortable with who you're becoming and trust others to accept and appreciate you as you are. Taking good care of yourself reveals that you can be loved and respected by others. Your healthy self-identity is affirmed and confirmed through new and renewed companionships.

Mutual respect includes trust and confidence in a genuine relationship. For this to happen, you need to understand one's moral character. Morals are the compass for all relationships. A relationship has certain limits, boundaries, and purpose. Every relationship has degrees and depths of meaning, whether casual, professional, spiritual, marital, familial, functional, etcetera. We'll explore the nature and value of friendships in the next chapter, which explores Step Eight.

Morals are the foundation for personal rights and wrongs. Knowing what's true makes you less likely to violate character strengths. Without morals, you can't make wise and healthy choices or decisions. You make yourself a victim of circumstances. Your moral voice is nothing more than a whisper in the wind. Choose the insight of Aristotle, who believed that virtue and good character are built on self-esteem and self-confidence.

Integrity occurs when you're open and honest. Others will doubt your sincerity and perceive you as a fraud and hypocrite when you fail to do otherwise. It requires moral courage. Undeniably, integrity is the vital connection between ethics and moral action.

Morality is primarily personal. Not everyone shares the same moral truth. There are many differences in moral beliefs. Subjects include sexuality, the death penalty, open marriages, assisted suicide, monogamy, heaven, hell, and the reality of God or a Divine Being. Beliefs may have a commonality, yet you may have relationships with those holding opposite ideas. The true morality test is the willingness to accept others with their "strange" convictions. However, there are exceptions to this attitude when their behaviors are pathological, criminal, abusive, manipulative, or downright mean in nature. These actions breach ethical principles.

The connection between ethics and morality is often confusing. Ethics are a system of principles governing morality. Your ethics are motivations based on ideas of right and wrong. It's a consensus of acceptable conduct in society. It's also consistent and reliable, not when it's convenient. Healthy relationships share common ethics. Ethical differences are the ground for unmanageable and dangerous relationships.

Albert Schweitzer claimed, "Ethics, too, are nothing but reverence for life. That is what gives me the fundamental principle of morality, namely, that good consists in maintaining, promoting, and enhancing life, and that destroying, injuring, and limiting life are evil."[36] Saint Luke says, "Whoever can be trusted with very little can also be trusted with much, and whoever is dishonest with very little will also be dishonest with much" (Luke 16:10, NIV).

Spiritual integrity stresses you love and respect yourself. In this way, you become independent, self-sufficient, and self-confident. You're experiencing the strength of spiritual health. You begin to understand how the fragmented parts of your past become whole. You stop the manipulations and con games. Your authentic self is maturing and blossoming.

Eleven

STEP EIGHT: GROWING AND CAREGIVING A CIRCLE OF FRIENDS

*We will remain open to ever-widening circles of loving friendships
and rely on the nurturing care of others without expectations.*

I was going through a period of depression. It wasn't the first time. On
other days, I felt isolated, lonely, and lost in the clouds of darkness.
During these "down" times, I detached and distanced myself from others,
especially those who loved and cared for me. I emotionally withdrew and
didn't want to disclose. When my wife asked, "Why do you remain silent when
I'm willing to listen?" I shrugged my shoulders, saying nothing. I could see
the hurt in her eyes. But I was caught in a void; I felt empty and had nothing
to share, much less give. My copartner and best friend knew the only way to
cope with my depression was to be present but not allow my emotional pain
to control her well-being. She had a plan.

A few days passed, and I came home from work; exhausted, I lay on our
sofa in the family den. I fell asleep but was awakened when I heard the door-
bell ring. My wife went to the front door, and suddenly, laughter and familiar
voices made me get up. I was amazed to see that ten of our closest friends
had brought dinner for all of us to share. They came to break bread with a

friend who was demoralized. What an act of grace, what acceptance, what affirmation. They were there as loving friends of presence with no expectations.

No questions were asked, and no answers were expected. We celebrated and toasted our deep friendship. We cried, laughed, hugged, and kissed. I went to bed, cuddled my wife, and fell asleep feeling the love and warmth of grace-filled friendships.

The next morning, I was filled with joy and gratitude for God's gift of friends. I found my copy of Henri Nouwen's book *The Inner Voice of Love – A Journey through Anguish to Freedom*. He affirms the power of friendship: "The friend who can be silent with us in a moment of despair or confusion, who can stay with us in an hour of grief and bereavement, who can tolerate not-knowing, not-curing, not-healing and face with us the reality of our powerlessness, that is the friend who cares."[37]

You need close friends who won't let you live with deceptions or reinforce negativity. Friends who love you despite who or what you do. Are you guilty of distancing yourself from such relationships? Do you resist being vulnerable? Are you afraid of exposing your tender soul? Have you built walls of false security and shut out those who will love you most? You're robbing yourself of one of life's treasures.

The Greek word for friendship, *philia*, refers to a freely chosen bond. While we can't choose our parents or family, we rise above our biological destiny in friendship. Mature friendships must be cared for and tended. This type of friendship is always open to growth and intimacy. Initially, friendship in this context begins like birth (newness and unknown). The infancy stage seems awkward and uncertain. You're excited about the novelty of learning and experiencing each other. Patience is a virtue that accepts the evolving dynamics of your relationship. Don't put time constraints on this growing process. Also, beware of unidentified expectations or desires. Searching for more intimacy or longing for more than friendship or sexual desires in the formative stage of new relationships may cause tension or distress. Remember the importance of a balanced relationship with mutual boundaries and limitations.

In Greek mythology, the great god Zeus ordered Hephaestus, the god of fire, to create the first mortal female to be beautiful, passionate, and curious.

Thus, Pandora (the all-gifted) was given some of their power by lesser gods, which could ruin humankind. Zeus sent these powers in a container with Pandora. She was instructed not to open the box. Zeus knew this wouldn't happen because Pandora was created with curiosity. Sure enough, Pandora became curious; looking carefully at the box, she picked it up. As Pandora raised the lid, plagues of countless sorrow and harm rushed for humanity. She clapped the lid down in terror, but it was too late. One good thing, however, remained there; it was hope.[38]

Pandora's box has become a modern symbol for hidden secrets or passions locked inside a person. You don't want to open this box for fear of what may be released. According to scholars of Greek mythology, such as Joseph Campbell, all myths are about the struggle of the Soul. And your soul is the seat of love. The struggle of one's soul is the fear of loving others as I am to love myself.

Christ tells us the first commandment:

"Teacher, which is the greatest commandment in the Law?" Jesus replied: "Love the Lord your God with all your heart and with all your soul and with all your mind. This is the first and greatest commandment. And the second is like it: Love your neighbor as yourself." (Matt. 22:36–40, NIV)

What's most intriguing about friendships is that they can occur between people with radical differences and similarities. Friendship doesn't require like-mindedness. In his delightful book *Soul Mates*, Thomas Moore assumes: "The soul can reach out and make its connections through and in spite of differences of politics, opinions, convictions, and beliefs. Friendship is the container of soul, not the process of weaving compatible companionships."[39] Moore believes friendship is not the union of personalities but a union of souls.

In this union, love happens; differently, it's called *agape* in Greek. This kind of love can best be translated as "holy love." Kahlil Gibran, in the book *The Prophet*, has this love in mind: "When you love, you should not say, 'God is in my heart,' but rather, 'I am in the heart of God.' And think not you can direct the course of love, for love, if it finds you worthy, directs your course."[40] Are you prepared to open your soul to this power of holy love? Dare you open this box and see what's inside?

Holy love isn't self-serving. It's an acknowledgment of your love connecting to God's uncontrollable love. Uncontrolling love is holy love. It deepens the sense of God's love in your life. You don't seek to control who another person is or what they do as a condition of your love. Agape love doesn't manipulate or set conditions for the love you give. It's the primal nature of God, Spirit, and Sacred Being in befriending human relationships.

In one of his more recent books, *Pluriform Love*, Dr. Oord states, "God's love is necessarily self-giving, others empowering, and, therefore, uncontrolling…God loves everyone and everything in this way. God cannot control anyone or anything."[41] While he doesn't formally use the term *holy love*, this is a common theme in almost all his books. God's uncontrolling love is the fundamental nature and manner of relating to all life. Therefore, "God loves everyone and everything" and empowers us to love and care for everybody and all creation.

A holy, soulful love requires you to reach beyond yourself. It's only through love that one is held blameless and made holy. Holiness is the surrendering of self-will and your responsiveness to God's love. The virtue isn't in loving another person but in loving as an acknowledgment of the divine worth of all God's creation. This sacred love is about all people, and its instinct isn't based on feelings; it doesn't run with pure tendencies nor spend itself only upon those for whom some sympathy is noted.

Annie was a shy, quiet child. She was born to poor Irish immigrant farmers. Her father was a troubled man as an alcoholic, and he physically abused Annie. Nurturing from her mother was limited because she suffered from tuberculosis. Annie was stricken with a bacterial infection at the age of five, which left her nearly blind. Her mother died when she was eight years old. Two years later, her father deserted Annie and her two siblings.

Annie was admitted to a mental institution. Doctors determined she wasn't treatable; the dungeon was the only place for the hopelessly insane. A nurse near retirement believed there was hope for God's children. She started taking her lunch into the dungeon and eating outside Annie's cage. Holy love transformed the life of Annie. The next year, Annie had surgery that restored most of her sight. She went on to graduate at the top of her class. The care and love of a human saint gave "little Annie" a dream and mission.

Annie became a young woman, and after more studies, she moved to Alabama. She was now known as Anne and was hired to be a governess to a six-year-old girl who had been left blind and deaf by an illness contracted at nineteen months. This young child had grown into an undisciplined, willful, and ill-tempered child with no means of contact with the outer world but touch. Anne had found her purpose and mission.

With patience and ingenuity, Anne Sullivan taught this child those things had names using a manual alphabet. Helen and Anne formed a sacred friendship that remained constant throughout the remaining years. Helen Keller and Anne Sullivan understood their friendship's depth and challenge.[42]

Literary genius Thornton Wilder believed, "There is a land of the living, and a land of the dead, and the bridge is love, the only survival, the only meaning."[43] Holy love is living with a soul sensitivity to the sacredness of all life. Love isn't something you do. Holy love is the unbridled power to be the healing agent of reconciliation to all of life's brokenness and senseless tragedies.

The depth of a loving friendship has complications periodically. Just because you seek meaningful relationships doesn't mean you won't have times when agony and suffering interrupt your comfort zone. Friendship doesn't mean codependence. It would help if you accepted that interdependence never overlooks self-sufficiency. Inevitably, any healthy relationship is not "clinging" or "insisting" on the care of another.

One truth I held in my younger years became a myth or falsehood as an adult. It was the belief that one person could fulfill all my intimacy needs, whether in marriage or deep friendships. How absurd! No person, friend, or soulmate has the energy or emotional strength to meet every significant need. I've discovered that my dearest friends are available in my pain and despair.

Authentic friendships are built upon risk and openness. It has a foundation of truthfulness and trustfulness. It's mutual giving and receiving. It's confirmed as well in what's known as communal fellowships. Fraternal groups, unions, and volunteer organizations, especially in the Church, are some examples of shared "community friendships."

Another communal fellowship is work-related coworkers. There are many interactions and maneuverings you will have to dance the "two-step" to avoid stepping on toes. Don't lose your balance!

Regrettably, sacred places of worship, akin to churches, synagogues, mosques, temples, or cathedrals, sometimes fail to be places of love, hope, faith, nurture, or kind fellowship. Spiritual and religious conflicts have a long history. In England, during the seventeenth century, a cobbler had a "saintly" pure heart; his name was George Fox. He witnessed unfriendly differences of opinion regarding doctrine and practice. He was disturbed by the hostilities and decided to rely on what he called the Inner Light. He challenged those who followed him to display a shared life of honesty, purity, and charity. They were to work for the cause of peace and the welfare of those in need. They were the founders of a group within the Christian fellowship known as Quakers, but the name they chose is officially known as "the Society of Friends."[44]

To be a society of friends displays the warmth you welcome visitors into communal fellowships. You show it by affirming each other across race and social class boundaries. You exhibit it by your affirmation of children and youth. You display it by your willingness to participate in sacred places that reach beyond the walls of a group or organization

Investing time and energy in communal fellowship is important to your spiritual health and wholeness. It's your choice and one that confirms your belief system. In the past, you may have been isolated or detached from such gatherings. Or you could have been a leader or victim of spiritual or communal abuse. You have either contributed to the divisiveness or shared emotionally and spiritually with those searching for God's presence and love to support them through their rivers of impossibility.

In selecting a communal fellowship, realize there is a difference between these associations and those with whom you want to be friends. You will freely have your reasons for the selections you make.

Communal fellowships typically have preset boundaries and purposes. There are social standards and behavioral norms for all who share this mutual gathering. It's also a fellowship where genuine and more intimate friendships can evolve. Some of your personal needs can be met and rewarded. Be cautious and sensitive to your boundaries and expectations with these "friendships." Stay alert regarding your emotional, mental, spiritual, and physical requirements for maintaining healthy relationships and caring for yourself.

Step Eight, caregiving, is a complex principle in developing loving and lasting relationships. It's evident when exploring the meaning and purpose of this kind of relationship. There's a general definition of "caregiver," which means supporting another person. To distinguish between caregiver and caregiving is the notion that caregiving commonly refers to a profession in human services. However, we will investigate a more inclusive understanding of caregiving.

The phrase used in this step states that we "trust in the nurturing care of others without expectations." The focus isn't on the nurturing care you receive but on the supportive care you give to those in need. American humorist Leo Rosten wrote, "The purpose of life is not to be happy, but to matter—to be productive, to be useful, to have it make some difference that you have lived at all."[45]

Agnes was a woman of strength and faith. At the early age of eighteen, she heard her call to serve God. With a holy heart and loving soul, she listened to God and consecrated her life by becoming a nun. When she joined the Irish Order Sisters of Loreto, she was named Sister Teresa after Saint Thérèse de Lisieux.

Sister Teresa received her first teaching order in a girls' school in Calcutta, India. There, she began her ministry to people experiencing poverty, for which she became famous. She once shared in an interview how she started her ministry the first time she cared for a poor, sick woman on the street in Calcutta. She claimed:

The woman was half eaten up by rats and ants. I took her to the hospital, but they could do nothing for her. They only took her because I refused to go home unless something was done for her. After they cared for her, I went straight to the town hall and asked for a place where I could take these people, because that day I found more people dying in the street. Within 24 hours we brought our sick and suffering and started the Home for the Dying Destitutes.[46]

Mother Teresa found a new order of nuns: the Missionaries of Charity. This was God's calling because of her love for others, her faith in Christ to sustain her, and her hope in caring for the hungry and homeless. Mother Teresa said, "I realized I had the call to take care of the sick and the dying, the hungry, the naked, the homeless to be God's Love in action to the poorest of the poor."[47]

Mother Teresa is the standard bearer of caregiving. But her depth of caring for others is more than most can give. There are many levels of loving care for those in their time of need. Sometimes, it can be as significant as a child seeing someone in pain.

Leo Buscaglia, an author, and lecturer on love, told a personal story where he is asked to judge a contest. The purpose was to find the most caring child. The winner was a four-year-old child whose next-door neighbor was an elderly gentleman who had recently lost his wife. Upon seeing the man cry, the little boy went into the old gentleman's yard, climbed onto his lap, and just sat there. When his mother asked him what he had said to the neighbor, the little boy said, "Nothing, I just helped him cry."[48]

It's common to have questions and concerns about caring for a friend or family member in need. Caregiving isn't always a matter of helping during sickness or distress. What you need to understand is that nurturing is compassion in action. Compassion's foundation is empathy. Being empathic can be stressful, especially when asked for physical and emotional support. Caregiving isn't predictable, and there will be concerns about the limitations and expectations you need to explore and define. You want to set and clarify boundaries with anyone for whom you care. It's comforting for both.

Caregiving includes meaningful interactions with different purposes. There are distinctions between compassion, empathy, and sympathy. Each one complements the other, yet you act and respond relative to the persons and situations involved. Compassion is your emotional response to another; you maintain your self-identity by understanding their feelings and circumstances without being consumed.

Empathy is your feeling of awareness toward others' emotions and circumstances. You attempt to appreciate how they feel. Empathy can make you intuitively more sensitive toward those who seem like you. You're not likely to link up with anyone whose familiarities don't reflect yours. That's because empathy comes from a feeling of sameness. One thing you have in common with others is being human. There are times when empathy may interfere with caregiving, at least subjectively.

Sympathy is your desire to help and be present during times of need. It refers to your willingness to be involved in someone else's feelings, mostly by knowing their sadness and pain. It's a more intimate connection, perhaps from your having similar heartache. Emotional and spiritual closeness can happen even when distance separates one another. It's energy that flows through the thoughts and feelings shared in love. Cherish the beauty of being connected through our hearts and souls.

Compassion, empathy, and sympathy provide the beautiful rhythm of mutual nurturing. They develop the tenderness and kindness that sustain your relationships. They don't have expectations or require reciprocal interactions. Nurturing has a natural flow of give and take. The fulfillment for you is knowing your love and care brings comfort and assurance to another. It's a simple but thoughtful tale (not true) about an administrator of a mental hospital. He is newly appointed to the position. He decided to get acquainted with patients, so he began daily walks. He would pause and introduce himself to each patient. One patient came up to him and said, "I like you more than the other administrator." "Why is that?" he asks. The patient, smiling, answered, "Because you're just like one of us." While humorous, the authentic truth was that the administrator understood the importance of caring for and nurturing those struggling with mental illness. He demonstrated the gifts of compassion, empathy, and sympathy with humility and kindness.

The spiritual well-being you seek is best experienced and affirmed when you're vulnerable yet committed to nurturing others. You bring stability, intimacy, emotional security, positive feelings, and self-validation to everyone because your heart, mind, soul, and physical presence are like the flowing waters of life.

This step emphasizes the need for nurturing without expectations. You care with mutual respect and accept the limitations of what you can do and when you can do it. You belong to the communal fellowship for a reason. It's a sharing community, and each person has special gifts to provide care for "friends" in need. No one person can or should be a caregiver. Exhaustion and stress are unnecessary side effects of overextending your desire to care.

Paul prayed for the Church to be a communal fellowship. He admonished his followers in his letter to the Romans:

> Be devoted to one another in love. Honor one another above yourselves. Never be lacking in zeal, but keep your spiritual fervor, serving the Lord. Be joyful in hope, patient in affliction, faithful in prayer. Share with the Lord's people who are in need. Practice hospitality. Bless those who persecute you; bless and do not curse. Rejoice with those who rejoice; mourn with those who mourn. Live in harmony with one another. (Rom. 12:10–15, NIV)

Living in harmony with one another is a challenge for anyone. It's natural to want conditions in a relationship. And those conditions surface with expectations. In what way do expectations, or the lack of them, confound your relationships? What's the expectation? A person's expectations are strong beliefs that you or others have about the appropriate way someone should behave or something should happen.

It's not helpful to demand unrealistic expectations. In communal relationships, where you are not free to determine the persons and parameters involved, you may hesitate to risk yourself. It's normal to be cautious. If you want your circle of friends to grow and enrich your life, consider how that can best happen. The centerpieces for all relations focus on compassion, empathy, and sympathy. But the depth and degree of your actions must be selective and realistic. Your investment doesn't discount your immediate needs or self-worth.

Mutual respect is significant to your caring connections. It's wise to predetermine your wants and needs before committing to others. Mutual understanding and acceptance accentuate the authenticity of your caring and support for each other.

Expectations shouldn't be rules or disciplines for behavior. Agree that there are limitations and conditions between you and your needs may not be met. It's mutual acceptance regarding the boundaries defining your connection. The world can be scary sometimes, and you may find days when you want to withdraw. Having friends and a caring support system can be demanding, even time-consuming. Self-nurturing is as important as caregiving. It would help if you had time to retreat and refresh. Beware of fatigue and exhaustion, feeling empty. Self-care means to embrace (hug) yourself and do something that fills your emptiness.

Twelve

STEP NINE: OPPORTUNITIES AND CHALLENGES

*We will seek opportunities for growth in daily service, trusting God
will give us the energy and strength to meet new challenges.*

Your spiritual quest will challenge you to grow to the next stage. The focus will explore broader and more profound degrees of service commitment. You'll experience emotional and physical opportunities to expand your knowledge and capabilities of being a whole person who broadens the circle of care and friendship. Some of you may have attained this level yet need to renew and refresh the effectiveness of serving others. Perhaps you may redefine or refine your understanding of helping others in need or committing to service opportunities that improve society.

"Opportunities of growth" refers to the process of spiritual maturity evolving developmentally. Growing your spiritual life is not restricted to these steps. However, you probably have learned so far that any growth is cyclical. You continue to return to some or all earlier steps for affirmation or confirmation of your self-awareness about your progress. All twelve steps build on each other.

Opportunities come from developing a keen awareness and being open to the guidance of God's Spirit. It's possible because your inner spirit connects with God's Spirit. God's Spirit serves as a mentor to you: "The Advocate, the Holy Spirit, whom the Father will send in my name, will teach you all things and will remind you of everything I have said to you" (John 14:26, NIV).

Opportunity includes timeliness. It's living within the urgency of each moment. It realizes the value of time and how you invest yourself. It's to understand that we live within a timetable, and time is not endless, at least for us mortals. Therefore, we must get serious about living each moment as if it were a lifetime. Quit postponing or waiting to do what is most important in your life. The New Testament says, "Yet you do not know what tomorrow will bring. What is your life? For you are a mist that appears for a little time and then vanishes" (James 4:14, ESV).

The Old Testament advises us to ask for guidance: "So teach us to number our days that we may get a heart of wisdom" (Ps. 90:12, ESV). The New Testament warns us to "look carefully then how you walk, not as unwise but as wise, making the best use of the time" (Eph. 5:15–16, ESV).

Please don't become a member of Procrastinators Anonymous; they have never had a meeting because it's postponed until tomorrow. Some people feel overworked, even burned out, so they avoid committing to anything new. They wait for more convenient opportunities. Caring for others can be time-consuming, though waiting for a timely opportunity may mean missing out on the blessing of the ordinary.

You intend to search for service daily. In this case, you're devoted to loving and caring for yourself and willing to serve others as needed. How is serving a part of your spiritual well-being? According to the dictionary, service is an "act of helpful activity" or a "contribution to the welfare of others." While this definition is "social" in nature, it's relevant for spiritual service.

Service is typically associated with a profession or defined services offered by a business or organization. Religious organizations (including churches, synagogues, mosques, etcetera) consider service essential to their ministries or agencies. However, "daily service" in Step Nine refers to the spiritual disciplines cultivating healthy actions advancing from one's soulful kinship to others.

This kind of service has the power to convert you. It can enrich your self-identity. It clarifies your perceptions and increases your sensitivity to caring for others. Your soul and heart are learning to have a sacred appreciation of servanthood. Humility and gratitude balance your blessings. The bonding is impressive and magical as you share your time in service with one another: "Therefore encourage one another and build one another up, just as you are doing" (1 Thess. 5:11, ESV).

You're budding and flowering in kindness in ways you never imagined. You attract friends and coservants who share in your spiritual presence. You're experiencing the spiritual high, the consequence of genuine sacrifice. The reality of sacrifice has a long history of true stories. An emotional one is about an eleven-year-old girl who asked her daddy, "What will you get me for my fifteenth birthday?" He said, "Please wait; there's much time left." Just before the girl celebrated her fifteenth birthday, she had a fainting spell and was rushed to the hospital. The doctor later met with the parents informing them her heart was failing and in critical condition. The parents went to visit their daughter, who was lying in bed. She softly asked, "Daddy…have they told you that I will die?" He replied, "No, you are going to live," as his tears flowed. But before he could leave, she asked, "How can you be so sure, Daddy?" As he was walking out the door, he turned and said, "Because…I know." While in the hospital, her fifteenth birthday arrived. After she left the hospital, she came home to find a letter on her bed that read, "My dearest daughter, if you are reading this letter, it means that everything went well, just as I told you it would. You asked me before turning fifteen what I would give you for your 15th birthday. I didn't know then, but my present to you was my heart."[49]

Service and sacrifice usually don't require a decision to give up a body organ or one's physical life. Granting such action requires a long discussion and mutual agreement before deciding. Legal and spiritual counsel is essential in considering these radical choices.

Being spiritually mindful, you sacrifice your desires to follow God's Spirit. Biblical self-sacrifice is the willingness to forget your own needs for the good of others. It's done not at the risk of ignoring your needs or desires. St. Paul declares, "You, my brothers and sisters, were called to be free. But do not use your freedom to indulge the flesh; rather, serve one another humbly in love" (Gal. 5:13–14, NIV).

Dr. Eugene Peterson's translation is more visual and prophetic. To interpret his imagery of freedom lost will confront your unhealthy impulses. He captures the intent and concerns of Paul. When one is ruled by selfishness, all kinds of corruption surface. You habitually are trapped in "repetitive, loveless, cheap sex," and your mind and feelings are "garbage." You grab for miserable, unfulfilling ecstasy. You're bitter and suspicious of everyone. Your unmet needs consume you, and you trust no one (Gal. 5:18–21, MSG).

You may have experienced this misery before adventuring to spiritual health. Whatever your past conditions, the future is open, and you can live in a new and refreshing world. One filled with the awesome blessings of God.

Your trust in God provides you with "energy" and "strength" to meet new challenges. It's one of the most exciting and daring parts of your journey. The spiritual life is a growing process, sometimes seemingly endless; you're not computerized. You're made of flesh and blood, with emotions. The prophet Isaiah confronted the people of his day, "But they who wait for the Lord shall renew their strength; they shall mount up with wings like eagles; they shall run and not be weary; they shall walk and not faint" (Isa. 40:31, KJV).

Your natural strengths can be discounted, and you may excuse your ability to reach new heights of caring and serving. Perhaps your memory of self-limitations is blinding you with past failed experiences. Or you're afraid of overextending yourself. You doubt or fail to trust God's Spirit to energize and strengthen you for new opportunities.

There's a universal philosophy that's more than a thousand years old, and it's called Taoism (pronounced "Daoism"). The Chinese tradition blends well with almost any spiritual/religious truth. C. S. Lewis discovered these beliefs and claimed he grew from being a Theist (a person who believes in the existence of a god or gods, specifically of a creator who intervenes in the universe) to believing in the God of the Christian faith: "Therefore, there exists an eternal, self-existent, rational Being who is the ultimate source of human reason. This Being we call God."[50]

Taoist teachings are primarily a guide to one's daily living. Lewis believed their greatest value pointed us toward self-exploration, growth, and transformation, which ultimately link us deeply to ourselves and the world. Lewis calls the Tao "the belief that certain attitudes are really true, and others really false, to the kind of thing the universe is and the kind of things we are."[51]

There's a contrast between being a survivor of pain or traumatic stress and learning to grow through troubling times. Discovering how your life is enriched through challenging times takes added energy, extra mental strength, and more clarity. It's the beauty of Taoism, for it guides you through difficult and intriguing periods of daily happenings.

Taoism is a process of teaching how to connect and balance natural and spiritual orders. It's the awareness and affirmation of how your body and soul are connected; thus, we're all spiritual relatives, sharing the adventures on this glorious planet we call home.

In the natural world, you feel a oneness with the magnificence of God's creation. Everyone is responsible for being stewards, protecting, and preserving this fragile and sacred earth upon which we stand. Genesis 2:15 (ESV) says, "The Lord God took the man and put him in the garden of Eden to work it and keep it."

Much of society insists that humankind isn't the steward of the environment but the benefactors. They argue that nature and all its creatures provide sustenance and comfort to us, the inhabitants. Everyone should read the passion of Pope Francis in his papal letter (2015) when he wrote, "The entire material universe speaks of God's love, his boundless affection for us. Soil, water, mountains: Everything is, as it were, a caress of God."[52]

Spiritually well-balanced individuals are receptive and grateful for the privilege and pleasure of sharing in the beauty of God's creation and the humble task of loving and caring for others. Let's not be naive about this challenge. Before you started this quest, there were ups and downs. During those days, you most likely felt depressed and lonely with little or no caring support. Prayerfully, you now understand there are positive alternatives to the old, limited options that confine you to distorted beliefs, feelings, and behaviors.

It's natural and normal to encounter complications in your relationships with others. It includes your most intimate relations, whether a spouse, family member, or dearest friend. Managing difficult and demanding interactions will test your "energy" and "strength" on occasion. Learning and practicing valuable coping skills prepares you for healthy and nurturing responses.

Taoism provides significantly helpful guiding principles. They're vital to one's spiritual well-being. It teaches how-to live-in harmony with the universe by following your natural impulses. Taoism focuses on healing, self-cultivation, and spiritual enlightenment through meditation and philosophical reflection.

Taoists believe nature is the most valid form of knowledge and wisdom. You learn this truth by living in harmony with the universe and following natural impulses. It's the art of living a simple life. You don't obsess over unnecessary possessions because they won't bring happiness or contentment: "Keep your life free from love of money and be content with what you have" (Heb. 13:5, ESV).

Simplicity is a core principle for spiritual wholeness. Today's social norms seduce you into thinking "more is better," and much more is "bliss." Reality? The more you own, the more you're owned. This increases your compulsive behavior to protect your possessions and way of life. Some believe that "gated neighborhoods" offer security and safety. National criminal statistics are increasing exponentially, and "gated" living isn't working.

The split of your mind–soul–body happens when you ignore the connection to God's sacred creation and your fellowship and friendship through the birthright we share. Scripture and other holy writings share similar teachings. You're here in this moment to live in harmony and balance with every aspect of your existence. You're a caretaker and caregiver to anyone and everything. Job held this belief:

> But ask the beasts, and they will teach you;
> the birds of the heavens, and they will tell you;
> or the bushes of the earth, and they will teach you;
> and the fish of the sea will declare to you.
> Who among all these does not know
> that the hand of the Lord has done this?
> In his hand is the life of every living thing
> and the breath of all mankind. (Job 12:7–10, ESV)

What's most interesting is the relevance in Step Nine of our need for "energy" and "strength" to grow spiritually. Taoism accents the balance between nature and our natural self. Scripture thoroughly emphasizes the nature of humanity concerning all of creation. In astrology, our birth date focuses on the four elements that are the basic building blocks of our world. Those elements are (1) fire is raw energy: bringing light and burning anything it touches to purge and create new life; (2) earth connects us to the tangible world and supplies the necessary resources to build our lives; (3) air fills our lungs, allowing us to communicate and connect; and (4) water cleanses, heals, and nourishes us.

The natural elements of life are evident in human nature. These basic elements of earth, water, fire, and air represent the physical and energetic qualities of the human body and the physical world. The ebb and flow of these essentials influence our physical, mental, and emotional well-being. They function in harmony. The wind raises the clouds to form the rain that nurtures the earth to grow vegetation, fruits, and flowers, and the fire kills diseases and insects that prey on trees and provides valuable nutrients that enrich the soil.

How do the four elements influence your spiritual well-being? They serve as powerful guides to living in synergy with nature. Every breath of air relaxes you. Fire gives you strength and energy. You learn to flow and be more fluid like water. The earth reminds you to heal and nourish yourself and others. When you align with the elements, you're more capable of tapping into the wisdom of life as God created. Therefore, you need to balance your spiritual and physical health. You're affirming that the wholeness of life can happen with a deep commitment to "daily" care. Running, exercising, praying, and meditating in rhythm, one with the other, is possible.

The Bible records Jesus's ministry and message using metaphors and parables connected to nature. In one such story, he paints the scene of a farmer planting seeds. Some seeds fall on the path, some on rocky places, some on thorns, and some on good soil, but only the seeds that fall on good soil grow into healthy plants. Jesus explains the story's meaning this way:

As for what was sown among thorns, this is the one who hears the word, but the cares of the world and the deceitfulness of riches choke the word, and it proves unfruitful. As for what was sown on good soil, this is the one who hears the word and understands it. He indeed bears fruit and yields, in one case a hundredfold, in another sixty, and in another thirty. (Matt. 13:3–8, 23, ESV)

The farmer's story illustrates how important God regards these relationships. The New Testament is the Gospel supported by the history of those called to follow and serve Jesus as Christ. The Old and New Testaments are accounts of how Creator God formed relationships with nature and, most significantly, man and woman. The spiritual life is the quest to know and serve God that develops over time. To grow in spiritual maturity is to discover and become the person God created you to be and become.

Why did God create you to experience this sacred journey? Who are you to be in this solitary moment of life? What's your relationship with the Divine? Who or what's God in your personal life? These are some of the vital questions asked in the Spiritual Inventory. Rain is showering on the fruits of your spirit, and the roots of your soul flourish in this awesome exploration of being and becoming.

Here's a summary of these questions. Genesis gives the account of God's creation of life in all its glory. God was pleased with the initial design but believed something was missing. Scattered throughout the Bible are clues about the reasons God made man. The first one occurs in a garden. Genesis 2:15 (ESV) says, "The Lord God took the man and put him in the garden of Eden to work it and keep it." God assigned him the task of being a caretaker for the earth. Adam was given authority over everything in that garden and beyond (Gen. 1:28, ESV). His authority was confirmed when God honored Adam by naming all the animals (Gen. 2:19–20, ESV).

What's important about the creation story? Creator God revealed the universe's purpose, especially male and female. God established the foundation for meaningful relationships by working harmoniously from the very beginning to accomplish Divine goals. Through many generations, from birth to rebirth, the narrative is recurring again and again. Ephesians 1:18 (ESV) verifies this: "Having the eyes of your hearts enlightened, that you may know what is the hope to which he has called you, what are the riches of his glorious inheritance in the saints." "Saints" means "holy." Being more inclusive, sainthood isn't limited to those with faith in Christ but anyone who lives with virtuous action inspired by faith. God seeks to have a personal relationship with you. The very nature of the Creator is love, and love is interpersonal. According to Thomas Oord, "Both God and creatures are relational. They affect others and are affected; their love is giving and receiving."[53]

When you search for energy and strength from God don't expect some magical elixir or tonic to boost your vitality. The health industry bombards you daily with the news of a new solution (drug) to your lethargy, fatigue, depression, or mental illness. You're tempted to buy into the commercial problem. There are countless bogus offerings guaranteeing you a better, even healthier life. It's called pandering.

The source of Hebrews offers advice for finding and obtaining spiritual endurance: "So don't sit around on your hands! No more dragging your feet! Clear the path for long-distance runners so no one will trip and fall, so no one will step in a hole and sprain an ankle. Help each other out. And run for it" (Heb. 12:12–13, MSG). This passage of Scripture verifies what it takes to face life's challenges. You're not alone.

God is present to you through the Spirit. The Spirit guides you and awakens your natural state. You have the innate power to tap into your inner strengths and capabilities. God loved you before you were born. Birth itself is the natural process of entering life through a mother's womb. Birth immediately connects you with airflow to the lungs, life-giving blood pumps through your heart, and energy and strength, filling your body with movement like dancing. God's pure love welcomes you to the Garden.

Dr. Oord reinforces this point: "God is present from the tiniest levels of life to the grandest. God is present to every cell, air molecule, and atom. God is present to every world, galaxy, and universe. God is present to each creature, great and small, including you and me."[54]

The God of my understanding is ever-present in all dimensions of the cosmos and the intimate aspects of daily life. God knows you, loves you, and is present with you in your daily encounters. However, God can't intervene or make decisions for you. You're to attend to your own life. Freedom is a blessing and a burden. It requires disciplined and committed care for your life. The Dalai Lama concurs: "A disciplined mind leads to happiness, and an undisciplined mind leads to suffering."[55]

Self-discipline is responsible for making persistent decisions that manage your behavior and actions, not emotions. It's an action without an impulsive reaction. It empowers you to be decisive and determined to follow through without wavering your decisions and plans until they are accomplished.

Commitment is a pledge to give your time and energy to something or someone you believe in. Commitment is the work of your heart and soul. Your passion and devotion are to be who and what you are with others. Say what you mean and do what you're dedicated to doing. You're dependable and can be trusted. Exercising commitment galvanizes relationships even when facing adversity. Failure to be committed will undermine your spiritual growth and health. It's made evident in the book of Revelation. We read: "I know what you have done; I know that you are neither cold nor hot. How I wish you were either one or the other! But because you are lukewarm, neither hot nor cold, I am going to spit you out of my mouth" (Rev. 3:15–16, NIV).

Sometimes the simplest and easiest way to reveal your commitment is through embracing the seemingly unlovable people who unexpectedly bump into you. Carl Jung called it "serendipity," which is a "meaningful coincidence of two or more events where something other than the probability of chance is involved." It's a moment of surprise and calmness. It's a chance meeting that can transform you and the stranger who "accidentally" enters your personal space without invitation. The following poem is a metaphor for commitment to the unexpected.

A Parable

His face is gnarled and weathered by the stormy seasons of life. His suit's wrinkled and worn from the sleepless nights on a cold park bench. Yet the old man's eyes sparkle with the sight of children playing. His ears perk up when he hears the clamoring of two squirrels tugging on a fallen acorn. He sits motionless, absorbing the sensations of the scenery that surrounds him. Looking down at his feet, with shoes that can't contain his toes, he sees the defeated squirrel who has lost the battle of the acorn. A withered hand reaches inside a tattered pocket, pulling out two stale popcorn kernels. Placing them in the palm of his hand, he gently offers a gift to his furry visitor. The tiny creature cautiously moves toward the outstretched hand, taking the meager offering as a token of friendship. The lonely squirrel peers into the eyes of the old man as if to say, "thank you," then turns, disappearing into the underbrush.

Glancing up, the aging, genteel face falls upon the eager smile of a small boy. The young lad, partially hidden behind an oak tree, has watched the tender encounter. He makes his way toward the pristine figure, curious about what gift he might receive. Again, a wrinkled hand buries deep into another pocket, withdrawing a piece of gum. The amiable fellow gestures to the child to accept his lean favor. Without a word, the cherub hand grasps hold of the priceless offering knowing the kindly man expects nothing in return. A touch on the shoulder signals mutual gratitude as the lad scurries off to share his joy.

The air is intoxicated with the fragrances of Spring. The sounds of laughter and conversation ring in his head. He is immersed in the warmth of the day, giving thanks for the *Gift of Life that is his.*[56]

Thirteen

Step Ten: Balancing Your Affairs and Attending to Lasting Values

We balance all our affairs and relationships through God's revealing presence to attend to what is of lasting value for sustaining spiritual growth in us and others.

When my next-to-oldest granddaughter celebrated her seventh birthday, she got a bicycle. She was excited and anxious to learn how to ride it. She asked me to teach her. That's something I did with some of my grandchildren. I remember the first bike my parents gave me when I was seven. I cherished it despite many falls and scrapes. They taught me the secrets of riding. Some were difficult to learn, but my mom told me, "Keep your balance; you're leaning too far (right or left)." My childhood instilled three fundamental beliefs about bicycle riding; I taught my granddaughter that day. I asked her to sit on the seat while still holding the bike. She wanted to "ride" immediately, but I insisted she be patient. I continued gripping the bike. She was frustrated and needed to know why I was waiting. I said, "Learning to balance is the hardest part of riding." When I let go, she began pedaling fast and yet leaning. I ran behind her, helping with balancing. But soon, she had her first fall. It was time to teach the other two secrets: turning and braking

119

without falling. She was a quick study. Riding was more fun than she had imagined. The joy of being a grandpa is priceless!

The word "balance" has many meanings. It's associated with business, economics, music, dance, gymnastics, psychology, yoga, and so forth. Balance signifies "to bring to or hold in equilibrium or poise." Fritz Heider, a social psychologist, developed a theory about situations involving psychological inequality. He called his idea *balance theory*. His notion was that we want to maintain psychological stability and form relationships that balance our likes and dislikes.

If one is sensitive and observant of our human condition today, there's a strong perception that we live in a time of severe imbalance. Many of us feel pulled apart, overworked, and exhausted. You don't have enough time on any given day to accomplish many things. Advertisements on numerous media formats promote the newfound drug or treatment to cope with the latest physical, mental, and emotional suffering.

Concerning spiritual health, you can't get a prescription, surgery, cure, or religious alternatives to resolve the imbalance. Why is this? Balance is the force that supports life; you experience it through your body, mind, emotions, soul, and spirit, all functioning together. It's the essence of well-being.

History and research have determined that many physical and mental illnesses are rooted in "spiritual dysfunctions." We've examined some of these in previous chapters. This chapter focuses on "balancing our affairs and relationships." Awkwardly, "affairs" has an illicit association with some presidents, popular media preachers, business frauds, and libelous actions of noted social people. Situations in this step involve personal experiences and relationships that have impacted you spiritually, emotionally, and physically. It's maintaining "balance" in all these transactions. Balance involves alignment: "Beloved, I pray that all may go well with you and that you may be in good health, as it goes well with your soul" (3 John 1:2, ESV).

Health and well-being are balanced. But not every day will you feel stable. Emotions are not constant; they fluctuate, so they flow with your negative emotions and attitudes whenever they happen. Anger, fear, depression, isolation, agitation, and so forth won't control you as in the past. Volition, not violation, is the creative power cultivating your strengths in caring for yourself and significant others. You need no longer become overwhelmed or feel "out of kilter." These uncomfortable feelings and thoughts can seem like a déjà vu moment with haunting memories.

Life itself is a natural balancing act. You're a combination of spiritual and physical beings. Stress and anxiety heighten when any part of you isn't in sync. You may tend to be concerned more about your physical condition. Conversely, if you ignore or discount the importance of your spiritual well-being, your physical health will suffer. There have been numerous arguments between writers and scholars, even today, who ask, "Are we spiritual beings having a human experience or human beings having a spiritual experience?" The only answer I can give is *yes*!

Relational balance has prerequisite feelings, emotions, actions, and spiritual principles. It requires being present, genuine, and contented in your body, mind, and soul. You experience personal enrichment that can't be measured. Fostering these balanced qualities affirms that you're taking better care of yourself, your family, and all those around you. The joy and fulfillment of living are equal when acknowledging God's Spirit's presence in everyday life. The Bible declares,

> As for the rich in this present age, charge them not to be haughty, nor to set their hopes on the uncertainty of riches, but on God, who richly provides us with everything to enjoy. They are to do good, to be rich in good works, to be generous and ready to share, thus storing up treasure for themselves as a good foundation for the future, so that they may take hold of that which is truly life. (1 Tim. 6:17–19, ESV)

"Truly life" affirms that we have a true self (also known as the real self, authentic self, original self, and vulnerable self) and a false self (also known as the fake self, idealized self, superficial self, and pseudo self). English psychoanalyst Donald Winnicott developed these concepts in the 1960s.[57] Our true self is capable of divine inner guidance to help us discover the fullness of life as crafted by God the Creator. Our minds and hearts long for self-love, self-respect, devotion, passion, joy, love, kindness, patience, and discipline, and our souls' faith strengthens us through this inner guidance. The dynamics of the Steps to Spiritual Wholeness help us develop or expand these qualities.

What are some of the dynamics in balancing your relationships? One of the primary actions is *harmony*. This emphasis is reflected in Taoism, whose yin-yang motif illustrates the dynamic process of balance and harmonization. Harmony is the emotional and spiritual affirmation of loving, accepting, inviting, connecting, compromising, resolving, and resonating with joy and gratitude in a relationship. There's inner peace and willingness to reconcile issues or concerns. You'll have times of disagreement or disappointment, but you won't get cornered in old reactions and responses. Trust in the healing process through harmonious actions.

Another balancing act is *loving detachment.* The idea of detached love comes from the Buddhist practice of unattachment, which isn't getting hooked on any thought, feeling, or experience. Attachment theory explains how you learn to bond with others beginning in infancy and how your attachment needs were met or not, affecting past and future relationships.

Loving detachment isn't tough love or loving from a distance. It's emotional and spiritual compassion, kindness, and honesty. It's genuine and direct. You feel grounded, guilt-free, and peaceful. Be comforted in this scripture:

> Love is patient and kind; love does not envy or boast; it is not arrogant or rude. It does not insist on its own way; it is not irritable or resentful; it does not rejoice at wrongdoing but rejoices with the truth. Love bears all things, believes all things, hopes all things, endures all things. (1 Cor. 13:4–7, ESV)

Loving detachment involves being sincerely present and attentive to others. You don't ignore or negate self-care. Caring for yourself is the positive strength of supporting the relationship.

We now transition to the subject of codependency. It's a topic with no shortage of authors having different thoughts. It can confuse anyone who has tried to break an addiction to another person or when a friend or family member has deeply hurt someone and still struggles to disconnect.

If you're fortunate to have had healthy parenting, you have the foundation to avoid codependency. The function of the maternal role is "bonding and filling a child's attachment needs." The paternal role is "detaching and helping a child to individuate."

How were your attachment needs met or not shaped who you are and have become today? Unfulfilled needs leave you empty and your love depleted. What are those needs? The caring and supportive attachments have at least three primary functions:

(1) Assuring a sense of safety and security. A child needs physical assurance verifying that their world is protected and predictable.

(2) Comforting emotions by soothing distress, promoting joy, and fostering a sense of calm. Every child needs to live in an environment free from anxiety and uncertainty. Feelings are comforted and accepted, no matter the child's or parent's mood or disposition. A loving warmth is constant.

(3) Offering a reliable and trustworthy base from which to explore. Children, by nature, are curious and adventurous, risking new experiences and unusual objects where hands and eyes delight in holding, touching, smelling, and tasting the unknown. Always encourage their "wild-eyed" vision of the world with discipline and wise counsel.

On the other hand, children need to discover and experience the strengths of detachment. Healthy detachment is letting go emotionally of the person or situation without ignoring or avoiding them. In this case, it's an emotional detachment from the mother. It helps the child discover self-care, self-identity, self-worth, and coping skills related to maturity. The presence and availability of a paternal figure teach one how to form positive relationships and friendships. The absence of a "father" can initiate "avoidance traits." Intimacy, kindness, caring, and loving are absent or limited. Or the child develops patterns of clinging, codependency, and inability to risk exposing oneself to vulnerabilities or fear of shame and loneliness. The greatest risk is never learning to feel, change, grow, love, or live!

While we've stated the importance of your relationships being balanced with harmony, we're not at the risk of denying or excusing the differences between each other. You may feel comfortable when you share similarities or common values. Variations are normal when dealing with race, ethnicity, social class, moral principles, spiritual beliefs, or professional practices. They can stretch mutual acceptance and challenge your willingness to be tolerant. It can be the most difficult action in sustaining meaningful relationships and friendships.

Tolerance confronts your biases, discriminations, narrow visions, rigid traditions, or injustices. Local, national, and international news headlines show the violence gripping our human communities worldwide. Human differences appear not to be tolerated. Tolerance isn't moral indifference or surrendering of personal standards. It's not shallow sensitivity to moral rights but respect for human dignity and frailty. In 1 Peter 3:8–9 (ESV), we read, "Finally, all of you, have unity of mind, sympathy, brotherly love, a tender heart, and a humble mind. Do not repay evil for evil or reviling for reviling, but on the contrary, bless, for to this you were called, that you may obtain a blessing."

God's Nurturing Spirit shows no partiality. But God's creative genius didn't make all of us "duplicates." We're distinguishable, and our brains have major differences in how we live and relate to one another. Perceptive parents know how to differentiate identical twins. Living with them and observing their behaviors and emotional attributes, they cherish their differences. Nothing is more intolerable than hearing a bigot claim, "They all look alike to me."

Some are arrogant enough to enjoy exhibiting their differences. They are convinced their "uniqueness" determines and deserves higher esteem and privilege. Dr. Stanley Hauerwas, theologian and professor, observes: "Too many of us feel that we have an adequate social identity because we hold 'right' views about matters such as ecology, feminism, racism, socialism, and wars. Such views seldom ask us to change our lives."[58]

Tolerance accepts differences, even if we disagree, and therefore, is considered a main part of the moral code of our founders. In the Bible, tolerance includes mercy. It has the implications of forgiveness, benevolence, and kindness: "But God's not finished. He's waiting around to be gracious to you. He's gathering strength to show mercy to you. God takes the time to do everything right—everything. Those who wait around for him are the lucky ones" (Isa. 30:18, MSG).

Let's now explore the second part of Step Ten: "Attend to what is of lasting value for sustaining spiritual growth in us and others." In the past and continuing in the future, you have formed legacies of spiritual, emotional, and physical values. Spiritual growth enhances your ability to deal with life's ups and downs and bounce back from those difficult experiences.

The value of managing your troubled times strengthens character and confidence in coping with almost any situation. Conflict and disappointment challenge you on any given day. An old saying, "Life isn't all sunshine," is a metaphor conveying the truth that life is a mixture of easy times, hard times, sunshine, and clouds. The great singer Ray Charles recounted the cloudiest day of disappointment when he tried out for Lucky Millinder's Band. He didn't expect to hear the words of Lucky when he said, "Ain't good enough, kid." Ray Charles said he brooded under a dark cloud for some time. After feeling sorry for himself, he spearheaded the cloud of gloom. "That was the best thing that ever happened to me," Charles recalled. "After I got over feeling sorry for myself, I went back and started practicing so nobody would ever say that to me again."[59]

Lasting values are your life experiences influenced by trials and tribulations. They become hard-wired in your mind, heart, and soul. There are multiple values, and you have read about many of them. "Lasting values" are those you spotlight most important in your daily activities. It's unrealistic to focus on all your values. Highlighting the primary values keeps you centered, your self-esteem affirmed, and you feel accomplished.

Core values are fundamental or foundational to every dimension of your life. They're the essence and testimony of your spiritual and relational principles guiding your true self. Identifying your core values can be meaningful when working on the Spiritual Inventory. Core values motivate and inspire you to reach out to others. They influence and govern your decisions and guide your actions.

You have or will pass down these aspects of your legacy from generation to generation. What values and beliefs have you inherited from your parents or parent figures? In what way(s) have you been influenced? Everyone typically has a personal list of centered values. They are critical to balancing your body, mind, and Spirit and maintaining healthy relationships. More importantly, by being guided by these values, your inner self remains assured, calm, and peaceful.

When someone claims, "I know to the very core of my being, what is true or most significant to me," they assume to have moral values that mold their life. Here are some common core beliefs worth accepting as foundational principles for spiritual growth in yourself and others. Having core or centered values connects you to everyone and everything.

It recognizes and accepts your self-values and doesn't mimic others. Integrity is the consistency of your actions, words, values, and moral principles. It's at the center of every true success. What's the core value of moral integrity? It's doing the right thing when no one is watching. It's a moral virtue and the basis of good character.

Spiritual integrity is being whole, including the quality of determined self-honesty. It requires significant self-awareness and an unbending commitment to be authentic. This kind of honesty is free from arrogance or blame. The cultivation of this kind of integrity comes from your heart and soul. No masks or pretending. King David lived by this principle: "Who shall ascend the hill of the Lord? And who shall stand in his holy place? He who has clean hands and a pure heart, who does not lift up his soul to what is false and does not swear deceitfully" (Ps. 24:3–4, ESV).

Another theme important to one's core values is that of companionship. It energizes and strengthens your spiritual character. You feel God's sacred presence when genuinely reaching out with spiritual and mental honesty. A sturdy spiritual center, not religious, gives you moral strength, the courage to hold your ground, state what you believe is decent and true, stand firm against inner or outer pressures, and not be caught in dread, even when fearful.

God has strengthened you to care for others in times of distress. Developing and maintaining core strength is a daily process. God's Sacred Spirit walks beside you, serving, loving, and helping others on this life's journey. The Spirit is your core strength. Isaiah tells us, "But they who wait for the Lord shall renew their strength; they shall mount up with wings like eagles; they shall run and not be weary; they shall walk and not faint" (40:31, ESV).

Companionship dodges social isolation and emotional loneliness. Building connections grounds you in strengthening meaningful relationships and reinforcing self-esteem. Companionship extends beyond close friendships or partnerships, sustaining social order and family structure. Sincere companionship is described in Acts 2:42–47 (ESV):

And they devoted themselves to the apostles' teaching and the fellowship, to the breaking of bread and the prayers. And awe came upon every soul, and many wonders and signs were being done through the apostles. And all who believed were together and had all things in common. And they were selling their possessions and belongings and distributing the proceeds to all, as any had need. And day by day, attending the temple together and breaking bread in their homes, they received their food with glad and generous hearts.

Reconciliation may seem like a word or concept that reaches beyond an individual's search for spiritual wholeness. However, you live in a social and communal world. You're engaged in various interactions daily. You're a social being created to live in relationships with others. Many years of my ministry and professional life centered on situations requiring reconciliation and restoration. I was an active first responder for tornadoes, meeting with victims of disasters and providing support to local respondents. I served in an inner-city ministry caring for the homeless and impoverished families whose crises included alcoholism and drug addiction.

The most difficult and heart-wrenching experience was being a first responder during the bombing of the Murrah Federal Building in Oklahoma City on April 19, 1995. I worked day and night shifts at "ground zero." I supported and counseled on-site equipment operators and all diverse rescue and recovery team members.

As a grief counselor, I assisted families and individuals to inform and confirm their loss of loved ones. I offered guidance and support in arranging funeral services. I conducted the funeral for the sister of my secretary and her family. The presence of friends and family included first responders who stood around the sanctuary walls with dignity and grace, offering their prayers and loving support.

The beginning of reconciliation, restoration, and healing embraced every victim, family, and countless "caregivers" who shared the pain and suffering of a tragedy that changed everyone's life forever.

The scope and power of reconciliation can be as simple as a hug and a forgiving heart. It's much more complicated and problematic when violence destroys life and death brings anguish and despair. The devastation can be brutal when racial or religious prejudice compounds hate and brutality.

You may be hesitant to become a "social" reconciler. You might be more concerned with circumstances closer to home. Your spiritual health most likely needs to be focused on fractured personal relationships. You may hope to restore a former connection requiring honest talk, forgiveness, and possibly self-sacrifice to achieve harmony and serenity.

Restoration or renewed relationships can be realized, but reconciliation is necessary. Restoration doesn't just happen without intentional decisions to repair and renew your relationships and friendships. Hold this truth in your heart and soul: forgiving and mending broken relations is possible because God the Creator first forgives and heals your life. The wonder and amazing strength of living with a restored, renewed, reconciled, and repentant soul is the discovery or recovery of the human community.

The *Washington Post* reported on June 19, 2015, of the tragic killing of nine members of the historic Emanuel African Methodist Episcopal Church in Charleston, South Carolina. The actual day was June 17, 2015. This report is an overview and a story of the aftermath of the bond hearing regarding the accused killer. A twenty-one-year-old man came to church that night to attend a Bible study. Various members welcomed him before he suddenly opened a shooting rampage, randomly killing nine members.

Some of the deceased's family members were at the bond arraignment two days later. Several spoke directly to the accused. Through their tears and deep grief, they spoke, not with voices of anger, but words of forgiveness. They let him know prayers for his soul would continue.

The newspaper report highlighted a young woman named Nadine Collier. She was the daughter of her seventy-year-old mother, one of the victims. She calmly but confidently said to the accused with humility, "I forgive you. You took something very precious from me. I will never talk to her again. I will never, ever hold her again. But I forgive you. And have mercy on your soul."[60]

My prayer for the worldwide human family is that we'll have the heart, mind, and soul of Nadine Collier. The suffering and agony of this faith community will take many years to heal. God's Spirit filled them with grace.

Too many would seek revenge, punishment, or retribution when experiencing tragedy. Forgiveness and mercy are making peace with your past. It doesn't matter who or what is the source of the breach. Forgive yourself before forgiving those who have harmed or hurt you. Reconciling is the beginning of a new future.

May everyone heed the wisdom and counsel of three world reconcilers. "A riot is the language of the unheard," and "darkness cannot drive out darkness: only light can do that. Hate cannot drive out hate: only love can do that" (Dr. Martin Luther King Jr.).[61] Nelson Mandela also said, "No one is born hating another person because of the color of his skin, or his background, or his religion. People must learn to hate, and if they can learn to hate, they can be taught to love."[62]

Repay no one evil for evil but give thought to do what is honorable in the sight of all...If possible, so far as it depends on you, live peaceably with all.
—Romans 12:17–18, ESV

These core values support the foundation of spiritual well-being. They're a select list; you'll want to reflect on your core values and their importance to your spiritual quest.

The Spiritual Inventory will help you identify the core values of importance to you. Allow time and space for meaningful exploration. Hopefully, you'll experience the renewing power of God's Spirit guiding you through unexpected and unimagined revelations.

Fourteen

Step Eleven: Delighting in Possibilities and Celebrating Life

*We delight in the possibilities of each moment of this day while
celebrating the rhythms of life with highs and lows, joys, and sorrows.*

Creator God's mastermind from the beginning designed human life for relationships. *Soulmates* are some of the most significant. Some would argue against such a notion. However, I believe in the predominant truth of our joy in being pet lovers. Pets are as distinct for any of us as one could imagine. Each one provides love and pleasure, giving comfort to our souls. In my experience, I discovered the delight of owning a dog as a small child.

My paternal grandparents were breeders of Boston Terrier dogs. They gave me a puppy on my third birthday. Our bonding was immediate, and we shared endless hours exploring our new world as pals. He opened my eyes and heart to the meaning of love and acceptance. More importantly, as I grew older and with other canine friends, they revealed (like various kinds of pets) that their style of loving and living differed from most of us human beings. I learned that most of the animal world enjoys the novelty of a new day. Excitement and exploration are the essences of their DNAs. They don't seek a purpose or reason to love. It's the very nature of most pets to care for you without condition. Life is "what" it is without asking "why."

Many animals are curious creatures and thrilled with unexpected treats or new adventures, especially with those who are their caretakers. They know when you feel pain or are lonely. They attend to your need for comfort or inner peace. Today is the only time that matters to them. Every day is a new day! Seize the moment for yourself.

This is the focus of Step Eleven. Discovering the possibilities of every day is delightful. Not being bored with the sameness of the day is exciting. Edith Ohaja is a teacher, blogger, creative writer, and poet, and her website is filled with inspirational thoughts and writings. One of her poems prompts us that "It's a New Day":

It's a new day, it's a new week
It's a time to trust and be blessed afresh
The hurts and disappointments of the past
may still be raw
But take a chance to open your heart
Open it up to possibilities of good
Believe that better things are in the wings
Things long desired
Things that will warm your heart
Embrace them from afar
Then pull them in by faith
It's a new day, it's a new week
May you experience the very best in it
And share same with everyone
The downcast, the crushed and heavy laden
Pull them up into the light
Put a smile on their lips and a song in their heart
Such that they can reach out to someone else
And spread the circle of love and light
Banishing the darkness inhibiting the

appropriation of the Creator's goodness
In Jesus' name.[63]

Open your heart and mind to new realms of reality. Let your eyes behold dreams never thought possible. There was a point in your life when it seemed mysterious and mythical. Days were filled with fears or boredom. Frequently, your life seemed hopeless and meaningless. You had little awareness of your life's purpose or the direction you were going. When you open your soul to God's Spirit, you will find new life, and the old passes away. The Spirit moves you into fresh and unrealized adventures. Your attitudes and behaviors are changed. The Spirit awakens you to stunning possibilities. Chaos is changed to creation. Roadblocks open into freeways. Relationships are restored. Races are reconciled. Hope rises from the ashes. Love happens in the most enchanted places, like families, cities, nations, and global communities.

At this point in your quest, there may be doubts regarding what is possible in your life. It's like reaching for the stars or imagining what is beyond the vast horizons of time. It seems novel, strange, illusory, even impossible. What matters isn't doing incredible things but doing simple, ordinary things, believing they'll be of immense value. It has been said, "When you know your weakness, you find your strength." Opportunities rise from the depths of insufficiencies. You've sometimes questioned whether life is more than you can handle. Simple things can be tough. You're convinced that you haven't been credentialed for much more.

The other half of Step Eleven encourages "celebrating the rhythms of life with highs and lows, joys, and sorrows." Whatever liabilities, emotional, spiritual, or physical pain limit your total investment in the "highs and lows, joys and sorrows" of everyday life, claim a new truth and write a new chapter filled with openness and potential! Sing with the Psalmist: "Delight yourself in the Lord, and he will give you the desires of your heart" (Ps. 37:4, ESV).

Socialized medicine is amusingly described as suffering people gathering to commiserate about their sickness. I can't take credit for the wit and wisdom of one who wrote, "Jesus can turn water into wine, but he can't change your whining into anything."

Paul's suffering was clarified to the church in Corinth, "Three times I pleaded with the Lord to take it away from me. But he said to me, 'My grace is sufficient for you, for my power is made perfect in weakness'" (2 Cor. 12:8–9, NIV). God's grace is the comforting strength supporting you through each moment of every new day. Grace is experienced the moment you walk into an accidental situation that God sews into the fabric of a routine event. It's an unexpected incident for creative action. You're in this place where healing and hope can happen. You didn't plan this situation, but someone is being blessed through your response to God's redeeming grace.

Will Campbell, a homespun Southern preacher, said, "Understanding grace does not send me into a state of inactivity and indifference. It sends me into the streets caring for humanity in response to grace."[64] Love isn't just a distinct way of feeling; it's an orientation of life and action. The Apostle John said, "Dear children, let us not love with words or tongue but with actions and in truth" (1 John 3:18, NIV).

Spiritual wholeness isn't a call to be an activist, protestor, or moral purist. Yet it would help if you were alert and engaged in maintaining a human concern for the well-being of others and all creation. Your will or intention stays motivated to care for those in need.

God extends an invitation to celebrate. Celebration isn't about being joyful. Research shows that people mindful of joy (celebration) feel more positive than those who obsessively expect happiness. The celebration is about the present. The clock of time is ticking; you only have this day to feel the gentle breath of the Spirit filling you with energy and passion for embracing all the options available.

How's this possible? Learning how to dance to the rhythms of life's music is compelling. What's astonishing about human nature is that your body, mind, and soul naturally gravitate to rhythm and movement. When you feel the vibration of liveliness, there's a sense of familiarity with the flow and ease of some days. On other days, you feel uncoordinated with anything or anyone. You are rekindling emotions and behaviors that are disabling. Remember, life isn't perfect; bad days happen. Concentrate on what has worked for you and guide you through tough times.

Advocates of positive psychology propose that you reframe what's happening now and pursue an attitude of positivity rather than relapsing to past failures. When you wake up each morning, take a deep breath, appreciate the pleasure of being alive, today can be filled with love and joy! Even Buddha asserts, "Each morning we are born again. What we do today is what matters most."

What does the rhythm of life indicate? It's a way of life that synchronizes your authentic needs, deepest desires, and unique talents. It's breaking the cycle of rigid habits and repeated patterns that have controlled you in the past. It's learning how to dance to the beats of your heart and soul. Sometimes, you may be so impulsive or impatient that you're unaware of the natural pulsations of your mind and body. Instead, you attempt to manipulate your thoughts and feelings toward personal ambitions, wants, and wishes. You don't trust the natural rhythms that throb through your very being, longing for deeper meaning and purposeful living. Some cellular biologists claim we are biological beings filled with "dancing energy." They assert that all creation around us buzzes with the sounds of life; your genes, brain waves, and cells vibrate. They stimulate your inner stirrings and a driving quest to discover fulfillment in living with an affirming purpose.

The adventure called life can be bewildering, confusing, and even complicated. Yet God's Spirit is the guiding force in helping us to define who and what we are to become. Celebrating life with a commitment to serve and share with others seems too general and undefined. Your purpose is more inclusive than having a vocation, profession, occupation, or career.

There's a difference between "having a purpose in life" and finding the "meaning of life." Discovering the personal meaning of your life is a reflective process, searching, through questioning or examining, for the significance of one's life. It's wanting to believe your life makes sense and matters. It can only happen when you're a contributor to your world. It's realized through relationships and those who affirm your investment in others. Living a meaningful life is essential to well-being and life satisfaction. Having no meaning has been compared to the feeling of absolute "loneliness." It's poetically expressed in the words of an unknown author and quoted frequently in sermons:

Loneliness is like a piano without keys,
like a violin without strings.

Like a sanctuary without a congregation
or a choir where no one sings.
Loneliness is like a blade of grass
growing through a crack of cement.
Loneliness is like a campground
without a single tent.
Loneliness is like a mockingbird
that cannot sing a song.
Loneliness is a feeling that one does not belong.
Like a pansy in a cornfield hidden where
no one can see.
I know all there is to know about loneliness
because it lives inside of me.[65]

Meaning involves examining the reasons and significance of your life in each day and occasion of making new memories. It's cherishing having a place and time to mean something to yourself, family, friends, and to causes that matter. It's accepting that you have the power to actualize your potential. You're not alone, and the journey ahead includes meaningful relationships. You care and are cared for.

Viktor Frankl, the Austrian psychiatrist, and author, was a prisoner in four different Nazi concentration camps. He knew the pain and agony of imprisonment. He discovered profound meaning during these painful times. He held that humankind's main motivation is finding meaning in life instead of striving for pleasure or power. Ralph Waldo Emerson simplified it best, "It is not length of life, but depth of life."

The prophet Micah understood God's meaning of life: "But he's already made it plain how to live, what to do, what God is looking for in men and women. It's quite simple: Do what is fair and just to your neighbor, be compassionate and loyal in your love, and don't take yourself too seriously—take God seriously" (Mic. 6:8, MSG).

In contrast to discovering the meaning of life, there is an inner desire and a deeper search for understanding who and why you are here. Most people want to know what the purpose of my life is. We want to have a sense of fulfillment. Researchers have learned there's a connection between living with a purpose and our fear that our death is meaningless. Investigators reported that persons were more than twice as likely to die prematurely as those who had figured out their purpose in life. They were more prone to having heart attacks or strokes.

One's craving for a purposeful life is unique to everyone. You've got a personal longing to know and accept God's gift of worthiness and to fulfill the intention of being a vital participant in this complex world. God's Sacred Spirit can unveil the passion stirring in your soul. You might sense your passion is hidden or, at best, lurking beneath the surface, waiting to be freed. When looking at different translations in the Scriptures, the words zeal and passion are interchangeable.

Your soul may feel like King David when lost in the wilderness of Judah: "O God, you are my God; earnestly I seek you; my soul thirsts for you; my flesh faints for you, as in a dry and weary land where there is no water" (Ps. 63:1, ESV).

You'll find a purpose in life when you awaken to the passion in your soul. The Spirit is continually breathing "fire" into your Spirit. The founder of Methodism, John Wesley, has incorrectly been credited for saying, "Light yourself on fire, and people will come for miles to watch you burn." However, he lived with such passion when preaching and throughout his ministry, like the prophet Jeremiah, who said, "If I say, I will not mention him, or speak any more in his name, there is in my heart as it were a burning fire shut up in my bones, and I am weary with holding it in, and I cannot" (Jer. 20:9, ESV).

I first learned about the topic of being a dominant right-brain or left-brain person in my adolescent years. I was taught everyone has a more prevalent trait than another. There's a common myth that "right-brained" people are more creative and emotionally adept, while their "left-brained" counterparts are more logical and skilled, such as math or calculations.

My mother graduated as a valedictorian in high school. My father only finished the eighth grade. Mom was smart. Dad was creative. I was a "scatter-brain," according to my parents. I was born in December. Sagittarians "like to go off the beaten path"; they are "Jacks-of-all-trades, masters of none." Math was my nemesis. My mom got irritated with my lack of ability. Creativity for me was pressure, trying to figure out what I "wanted" or how to do it. Dad asked me to help with "projects," but he never had the time to "teach" the craftsmanship. However, I learned a lot watching and assisting him.

Searching for my life's meaning and purpose became a journey down twisting roads and troubling waters. I was confused and lost in a world of mystery and misunderstanding. Drugs never tempted me. My parents were strict, and my dad was the disciplinarian. I was a quick study; I didn't act out. I became obsessive and compulsive to find my own talents and interests. Those included music, acting, debating, and involvement with social and religious groups. I kept my mind and time busy. But I stressed over what was the meaning and purpose of my life. I had no answers during this period.

I was honored and praised for my talents and gifts. I received outstanding awards and earned college scholarships. Like high school, I focused on music, drama, and debate. I graduated with honors and awards and received a full graduate scholarship to seminary. I accepted it, not intending to be clergy, but perhaps a professor. Being naive and immature, I thought I had worked hard and deserved such credits.

In my middle year of graduate school, I experienced a spiritual awakening. I learned it wasn't my obsessive-compulsive nature driving me but God's Spirit leading my heart and soul with passion. I recognized and acknowledged that passion, not my ego or personal talents, was an energizing force. God unveiled my mind's self-conceit rather than the spiritual gifts to share with others.

The Spirit gave me an unclouded vision of the meaning and purpose of my life. The faculty selected me as Outstanding Preacher of the graduating class, another affirmation of God's gift of passion for fulfilling my reason for being.

What stirs your soul? What keeps you feeling alive and energized? Focusing on the interests and activities that capture your heart and soul can bring you closer to your true passions. Do you have a clear view or idea of your life's direction? Do you have worthy goals, and are you devoted to them? Or are you wandering with no appealing or desirable goal in life? Listen to St. Paul's encouraging words to the church in Corinth, "So we do not lose heart. Though our outer self is wasting away, our inner self is being renewed day by day" (2 Cor. 4:16, ESV).

Fifteen

STEP TWELVE: AFFIRMING GOD'S RENEWING PRESENCE

We live gratefully and graciously, affirming God's renewing presence in all we greet today.

Knowing God's presence can only be experienced when you have a healthy understanding of Who God is. Many people have formed assumptions about God and imagine they believe in the One, True God. Our focus won't be on false gods (idolatry). We'll uncover some of the countless false beliefs about God as Creator, Redeemer, and Revealer. Traditionally, the Trinity is termed God the Father, the Son, and the Holy Spirit. Historically, there have been wide chasms of teachings and views regarding the nature of God.

Ecclesiastes warned those who make wrong notions about God: "Fools base their thoughts on foolish assumptions, so their conclusions will be wicked madness; they chatter on and on. No one really knows what is going to happen; no one can predict the future. Fools are so exhausted by a little work that they can't even find their way home" (10:13–20, NIV). Some are false teachers regarding God. Others have distorted or misinterpreted the actions of God and the biblical messages. I acknowledge there'll be critics and naysayers about the Twelve Steps to Spiritual Wholeness as presented here. I'll undoubtedly approach one's understanding of God and the meaning of spiritual teachings more broadly and inclusively than many. My intent isn't to challenge or change your spiritual foundations or beliefs. I'm hopeful you'll be open to exploring and experiencing a panoramic perspective of spiritual health and wholeness. Let your heart, mind, and soul consider different options and more adventurous paths to a new life. You're the only one who can validate the journey. You'll discover and confirm what's "truth" for you in this transformation pathway.

We'll consider two realms of faulty assumptions in the Twelfth Step. They're related to one's personal or self-assumptions. The other element is the mistaken spiritual assumption regarding the power and relationship of God in every dimension of life. Experience or lack thereof has influenced your views, habits, and actions regarding spiritual convictions or principles. They're at the center of your life map, as discussed previously.

Time and space limit us in identifying only a few of these assumptions. You may consider adding your assumptions to the Spiritual Inventory. Addressing assumptions about yourself, loved ones, friends, and others is crucial to loving relationships.

There are volumes of resources about false assumptions. Still, the importance of this subject to spiritual health is undeniable. An assumption is something you think you know without questioning it. And your assumptions may be incorrect, and they're the source of pain and estrangement. Daniel K. Held is an ordained clergy and licensed therapist. In his essay, "So What Happens When We Assume?" his professional wisdom reinforces such harm:

> I've found the #1 ingredient in a loving and helpful relationship to be accurate understanding as produced by successful communication. And the #1 cause of a failure to communicate is an unquestioned assumption. Assuming an untruth about another, be it a spouse, a child, or anyone else is anything but loving or helpful.[66]

Self-assumptions include visions, beliefs, and change. Our brains are wired to make assumptions because the absence of experience and knowledge intuitively compels us to decide or choose. Often, what we envision is off base. We think it's an honest mistake; science calls it a blind spot. Unconscious biases distort your vision and impact your behavior.

Life, at times, seems to be an experiment. There are science fiction advocates who support this possibility even with the absence of any truth. There's constant scientific research studying the origins of life on Earth. Some seek evidence that Earth, and all life on it, is an experiment by some advanced alien civilization.

My vision and conviction are the reality that, God the Creator, is the author of life, even when considering the Big Bang theory. There's meaning and purpose in every dimension of life, natural and human. Life isn't so much an *experiment* as an *adventure* traveling down uncharted paths.

Your outer vision allows you to see the world around you, and the inner vision provides spiritual insight. How do you see yourself? How do you want to be seen? Have you molded a hollow image of who and what you are? Do you desire to be an authentic self? Healthy visions don't get trapped in idolizing another person's visions, values, or beliefs. Allowing yourself to imitate someone you admire at the expense of ignoring your sense of truth is *self-denial.* The outer and inner vision reveals your authentic self. It's not about perfection; it's recognizing and accepting your flaws, deceptions, and limitations. Vision from this perspective is opening your heart to the truth that you matter and claiming the right to live your life filled with joy, love, and spiritual blessings. In the words of John Denver, "Some days a diamond; some days a stone."

Visions can be myopic, meaning nearsighted or farsighted. It's demonstrated by your lack of awareness about the difference between one's false and true self. Logically, your false self was formed from wrong assumptions and warped concepts. Naturally, it feels comfortable because it's automatic, predictable, and rigid. Sigmund Freud called it "repetition compulsion."

Psychologically, the false self is connected to the real self. It inflates, mocks, simulates, and offsets it when we lose contact with our true selves. It also links us to our history from birth. The natural real self is intuitive, inspired, fluid, pliable, free, and boundless. Your self-vision's value and importance must be balanced with your beliefs. Beliefs are the anchors defining how you live and breathe in this world. They ground your actions, behaviors, and living presence in the real world. Beliefs, like vision, are composed of false and true factors. An assumption is something that's accepted as right but not proven. A belief is when an assumption is confirmed true or held with more conviction. Assumptions affect your perceptions and beliefs impact your behaviors. Mark Twain and many others are credited for saying, "It ain't what you don't know that gets you into trouble…it's what you know for sure that just ain't so." Seems plausible!

Long-held beliefs and assumptions are responsible for much of the violent and irrational behavior in the world associated with racism, religious bigotry, fundamentalism, and ungodly notions of false "gods" who support "selective" groups and organizations. These people and groups imprison the very people whom God loves and redeems! When you create new visions and beliefs, you will encounter life changes never imagined when you live these new visions and beliefs. But first, identify false assumptions about yourself or your identity that are distressing you. Most of us aren't privy or aware of our assumptions or beliefs. They're so ingrained in our psyche that we consider them the natural components of daily living. I will suggest some bogus beliefs.

1. **I am unlovable because I don't feel loved.** Do you believe you deserve to be loved since you try to love and accept others? Is receiving love a reward? In what ways do you want to be loved? The truth about love is that it's not a *feeling* or an attitude. Love is a decision to care for others; it's action minus expectation. Like God's grace, it's unconditional.

2. **Love can control others.** Daniel Held's essay explains this false assumption: "Love empowers others' truth as a better alternative than a lie. It will never decide for others who, by God's creation, are already capable of deciding for themselves. Love's power is in its ability to multiply by empowering others to control themselves better."[67]

    There's a problem when love is manipulative. Many people use love as a means of selfish gain. Compounding love with feelings is confusing it with our senses. Feelings have all levels of intensity and fluctuations. It's the mistaken view that sensual attraction is love.

The true nature of love is the desire to share your well-being with the well-being of another. Relationship barriers are overcome when you welcome the presence of someone into your circle of love and vice-versa.

A healthy and open love doesn't control. It doesn't dominate, overpower, or force. The Apostle Paul put it simply in 1 Corinthians 13:5 (ESV): "[Love] does not insist on its own way." Therefore, love is its own reward or compensation. Let go of your illusion that a significant other will want to change if your love is deep and lasts long enough. How fruitless and exhausting!

3. **Seeing every challenge as an obstacle that is impossible to overcome.** This assumption is victim-focused. Opportunities gone, missed out. Possibilities denied, not qualified. Others are more capable or deserving. The future seems dim and dismal. Reality sometimes sucks!

Do you sense that a dark cloud hovers overhead? Were you born under the wrong sign? Is success a lie? The word hope has no meaning for you. Hopelessness is a feeling of despair usually associated with depression. More often, it's false assumptions painting your world in darkness. Failures rather than victories are your life's resume. Life combines disappointments, losses, alienation, frustrations, and defeats. Having hope is a healing power to address these distressing times. Psychologically, hope is a positive state of mind built on anticipation of assured outcomes concerning incidents and conditions in one's life or the world. Spiritually, it's the confident hope based on faith. Faith and hope function in harmony. Faith is grounded in the reality of the past; hope is looking forward to the reality of the future. Here's a familiar truism: "Without faith, there is no hope; without hope, there is no true faith."

How do your assumptions alter one's character? How can your well-being change when acting on false assumptions? Nothing. You're blocking the possibilities about new experiences, renewing old relationships, or discovering new ones. You're repetitiously imposing tough decisions or preventing thinking outside the box. You're imprisoned in a vacuum. Boredom tends to control your life. Every day feels like a rat race around his cage. Your energy dies, and joy is dormant. To jump off the whirling cage, you first want to stop the habitual and fruitless behaviors compulsively driving you. What are some practical options for living without false personal assumptions? Seeking the truth and facing reality isn't simple or clearly defined. You have attempted to overcome or ignore the lies in the past with little success. Or you haven't recognized or sensed the need to change until now.

False assumptions are learned and conditioned thoughts and behaviors. Life experiences create memories. Memories form beliefs and values. You've spent years confirming what's factual in your maturing life. There has been no reason to question your assumptions because they have structured your life and helped to control your world.

Doubt is your ally. Questioning is your freedom. Courage is your action. Faith is your hope. Trust is your power to change. Change opens the doors to uncertainty. Finding your true self is impossible until you admit you're lost and your actions aren't working.

The human brain has a lengthy evolutionary history. One of the basic functions is the "survival" mode. In an unstable world, our brains naturally seek to stay alive and be safe as best as we know how. The more complicated and abusive society becomes, the more relationships co-mingle with those who share common assumptions.

First, free yourself from cultural assumptions that keep you bound to conventional social ethics and principles. In this case, crowd identity is more important than your self-identity. Acquaint yourself with the true self that has been isolated and insulated from reality through faulty beliefs and associations. Identify whether the assumption is your belief or if you're mimicking someone else.

Second, question the validity of your assumption. Is it based on facts or biases? Is it grounded on past experiences? Or intense feelings? Check resources to ensure you know what is true. The questioning technique challenges assumptions, reveals contradictions, gains new knowledge, and increases wisdom. You may be enthusiastic about an assumption, and your assessment finds it reliable. Risk unwrapping its suppositions. Not all assumptions are fact-based. Many rely on feelings, and others on faith. The stronger your feelings, the more resistant you may be to change. Recognize and affirm these forms of assumptions: "Now faith is the assurance of things hoped for, the conviction of things not seen" (Heb. 11:1, ESV).

Third, communicate openly when you're interacting with others. Let others know what you claim to know. Be sincere in receiving another opinion or asking for clarification. Avoid prefixed ideas or stubborn attitudes. Trust your mind and heart to learn new options about changing. Realize and recognize all the possibilities presenting themselves to you.

Fourth, learn and practice "mindfulness" to live a meaningful life. How does this theory relate to assumptions? In the teachings of Buddhism, mindfulness shows us that separation is an illusion; our belief in an independent self is imagined. We're connected to each other and all of nature. These are true assumptions that unite us and create concord.

Mindfulness is the focus of one's inner vision. It's the power that releases your true self to actualize your innate capacity to accept others with their differences, beliefs, and values. Mindfulness brings a gentle and compassionate way of being with yourself and others.

Mindfulness helps your brain focus and concentrate on the immediate problem or situation. It allows you to have clarity when assessing your assumptions. It keeps your thoughts and actions in the moment. It dispels confusion and uncertainty regarding what actions or behaviors mobilize you.

The essence of mindfulness is how you breathe. The ancient Greek word *pneuma* means breath, the energy of one's spirit or soul. Shallow breathing indicates uncertainty, anxiousness, and even phobias. Deep breathing occurs, filling you with power and strength. It awakens, stirs, moves, calms, and sustains you through all moments of your life. Release the tension. Relax in the present. When your breath is shaky, all is shaky; when the breath is calm; all is calm.

We'll now shift to a more intriguing assumption. The God assumptions are vast, and many are disruptive. There are false assumptions about God and false prophets who portray God with personal interpretations that harm those who seek to know an unknowing God, Spirit, Redeemer, or Holy Presence. We'll unravel and explore a few of these beliefs or untruths. Again, our attention isn't on false prophets who fabricate truths about God and are narrow-minded and mistaken. We'll consider and appraise how some teachings about God are adopted through human experience, misinterpretation, or misunderstanding. I will only concentrate on what I consider the most notable false assumption:

God controls what happens in life, whether good or bad: "Don't be deceived, my dear brothers and sisters. Every good and perfect gift is from above, coming down from the Father (Creator) of the heavenly lights, who does not change like shifting shadows" (James 1:16–17, NIV).

There's a theological theory called *omnipotence*, defined as "all-powerful." Normally, it's linked to the belief in *omniscience*, implying "all-knowing." It's the perception of God as absolute; there's nothing before or beyond the power and knowledge of God. I won't venture into an explanation of this belief in this book. I'm interested in how God's nature is related to one's spiritual growth and health. Deceptive assumptions are dangerous to spiritual well-being and practices.

This specific assumption about God complicates and confuses one's ability to "affirm God's presence to others." We're not discussing "denominational doctrines" or world religions' differences in teachings. "Spirituality" has a universal appreciation for truth and meaningful connections to all dimensions of life, natural and human.

A "controlling" God who interacts with you through "controlling love" can't be nurturing or supportive. If God is all-powerful and all-knowing, then free will is a myth. Grace becomes conditional, and forgiveness is pointless. If Christ is God in our living presence, how do we understand his compassion, companionship, testimony, and human sacrifice for others? He lived by the principles of "uncontrolling love." The Greek word for this love is *agape*, an open and relational dynamic. In Scripture, the supreme agape love is the highest form of love, contrasted with *eros*, erotic love, and *philia*, or friendly love. The shared love between God and humans is evident in one's unselfish love of others.

Paul depicts the spirit of "uncontrolling love" in 1 Corinthians 13:4–7 (ESV): "Love is patient and kind; love does not envy or boast; it is not arrogant or rude. It does not insist on its own way; it is not irritable or resentful; it does not rejoice at wrongdoing but rejoices with the truth. Love bears all things, believes all things, hopes all things, endures all things." The dynamics of this kind of love hold God and humans to the highest standards of uncontrolling love. We're accountable for our choices and decisions. The idea that God is all-controlling distorts the issues of evil, suffering, tragedy, and nature's ever-present devastations. Some argue that God's intent for any suffering or misfortune can eventually have a positive outcome that can ultimately enhance growth. This concept of God doesn't control the situation or the outcome. It violates God's nature of love and caring.

Again, Paul says we have a "God of all consolation who consoles us in all our afflictions" (2 Cor. 1:3, NIV). Dr. Oord's view of empathy is this: "God's heart breaks by what breaks us. But this heartbrokenness does not lead God to despair…God's sensitivity and emotion never lead to evil, because God's nature is love…God responds to all that is negative, frustrating, and painful with resilient hope."[68]

There are many portraits of God as Sacred Being, Creator, and Father. One of my favorites is in author William P. Young's novel *The Shack*. I didn't read the book but saw the movie. It's the story of a man named Mack, who falls into depression following the death of his daughter, Missy. He receives a strange letter inviting him to a deserted shack in the Oregon wilderness. Reluctantly, he goes, not expecting to meet (Young's depiction of God) an African American woman named Papa, who whips up great comfort food and zesty dialogue.

Papa breaks many of the disillusioned beliefs about God. She is warm, funny, and relatable. Mack learns important truths about his daughter's death after her body is found. It transforms his understanding of the family tragedy and altered his life forever. Mack's view of God is radically converted, and he welcomes the kinship with God as "Papa!" There's no question that human suffering and tragedy can change you. There'll be significant insights and renewing life experiences. But it doesn't mean God is the source or initiator of your grief or human agony. God feels your pain and provides the means for healing.[69]

When you learn and accept that your true (authentic) self-embodies God's divine nature, you can easily recognize you're more than a physical body. You have a divine consciousness that connects your spiritual self to the eminent presence of God's Spirit.

The central theme of Step Twelve is acknowledging God's creative gift of living your life in the fullness of all that surrounds you. Your mind, soul, spirit, and body are the channels and conduits through which God opens you to the wonders and beauty of nature and the amazing possibilities of sharing in the sacred sanctuary of the human family. My hope is in a meditation I wrote many years ago when I celebrated the births of my three daughters. My sentiment after the birth of each grandchild still stirs my heart and soul.

Pure Vision

She smiled with angelic innocence. Her tiny hand, smelling of perfumed powder, gently patted my nose. Her wee voice uttered wordless sounds in my ear. What pure love could be more profound than this moment? Forget that she was my daughter. Ignore my pride in knowing she was special. At this moment, I was experiencing the amazing grandeur of God's creation.

We are created to reach out and touch one another's souls with sheer, chaste love. We are to live with an angelic innocence whereby we judge no one or expect the worst. I am not speaking with naivete, for there are cruel people in the world. Yet we are called to live by faith and the absolute trust that we can love unconditionally.

And the greater challenge is to love unreservedly. I had forgotten how to look at others through the eyes of a child. I don't remember when I smiled and gently held someone, believing they would graciously accept my gift of love without conditions. Oh, I have done this with my family. However, I seldom do this with others. How about you? Today, let your inner child be free to express your life's deepest feelings and fondest hopes. At least take a few minutes risking, being open to giving, and receiving the remarkable gift of God's grace. Smile, like the sun's warmth, and provide even a stranger with the overwhelming miracle of being special.[70]

Conclusion

A friend asked me what my book was about. I had no immediate answer, but I did ponder the question. After some reflection I told him the underlying themes were paradigms. Thoughts and ideas requiring new perspectives. Recognizing illusions and myths that need fresh templates and alternatives to experience spiritual health and wholeness.

The primary premise of this book is an affirmation that God as Creator, Sacred Presence, and Holy Comforter is made manifest in human and natural relationships. We aren't solitary beings cast upon a boundless sea or into a mysterious wilderness. We're on a spiritual journey that has purpose and meaning through our connections with all creation.

Our humanity and divinity are rooted in a loving God who is on the same journey with us. In our darkest moments and enlightened events, we're not alone. But knowing how to live in relationships is the challenge. Initiating new relationships has its own set of stressors. There are fears of rejection, fears of being vulnerable, risking self-disclosure, and the whole process of trusting someone you know little about.

However, the process of maintaining and sustaining important relationships can be even more stressful. But healthy relationships are never sacrificed at the expense of tension and times of struggle. Valuable relationships are born from the agony and ecstasy of mutual commitment. We covenant together to be unified in all that is required to share life with each other. I've a sincere desire and prayer that this book is more than a one-time read for many of you. The *Twelve Steps to Spiritual Wholeness* is a process of learning and imprinting. An imprint is a belief system or a deeply embedded memory that has altered how you see yourself, someone else, or the world.

The Soul Quest hopefully has a lasting impression and will be a spiritual companion and guide as your life expands and reaches the magnificent horizons welcoming you to a new day and new life.

Prayer for Today

God, O Holy One, give me the inner peace and outer vision to live each moment of this day with the exciting possibilities of the unknown and unplanned. Help me release the control I require over my life and the people around me so I can discover the freedom of Your Living Presence. Amen.

Acknowledgments

This book would never have been written without the loving support of dear friends, colleagues, and my family. It's the result of many years preaching, teaching, lecturing, counseling, and being a first responder to tragedies and broken dreams. God has given me the heart and strength to be present in times of need. Many blessings and lasting comfort abide with me and prayerfully with each one whom, when, and where we met.

Twelve Steps to Spiritual Wholeness

1. We admit we are powerless to change the lives of others and we will accept the responsibility and consequences of personal choices we make.
2. We believe and will trust in a creative and interactive God who can restore us to spiritual wholeness and empower us to grow.
3. We will freely respond to God's spiritual guidance and faithfully act upon the decisions we make through spiritual discernment.
4. We acknowledge our self-defeating behaviors and seek God's wisdom in becoming the self-actualizing persons we were created to be.
5. We will make a sincere spiritual audit of our lives and accept God's grace-filled power to heal our inner brokenness.
6. We will take a leap of faith and disclose our inner selves to others to acknowledge God's acceptance and forgiveness of our lives.
7. We claim in humility our God-given gifts, and we will joyfully share who and what we are as we build caring support for ourselves and others.
8. We will remain open to ever-widening circles of loving friendships and rely on the nurturing care of others without.
9. We will seek opportunities for growth in daily service, trusting God will give us the energy and strength to meet new challenges.

10. We balance all our affairs and relationships through God's revealing presence, to attend to what is of lasting value for sustaining spiritual growth in us and others.
11. We delight in the possibilities of each moment of this day while celebrating the rhythms of life with highs and lows, joys and sorrows.
12. We live gratefully and graciously, affirming God's renewing presence to all we greet today.

Endnotes

1. Laurie Buchanan, www.tuesdayswithlaurie.com/. Reprinted with Permission.

2. Ronald Rolheiser, *The Holy Longing: The Search for a Christian Spirituality* (New York, Doubleday, 1999).

3. Ralph W Emerson, Waldo *(2010). Collected Works of Ralph Waldo Emerson, Volume VIII: Letters and Social Aims,* Harvard University Press. 191.

4. Sam Keen, *Hymns to an Unknown God: Awakening the Spirit in Everyday Life* (New York, Bantam Books, 1994). 5.

5. Erich Fromm, *War Within Man: A Psychological Enquiry into the Roots of Destructiveness,* Pamphlet for US Quakers (1963). 5.

6. Albert Schweitzer, "Reverence for Life," www.en.wikipedia.org/wiki/ Reverence for Life. Accessed 5/21/2022.

7. *"What is the Difference Between the Mind, Spirit & Soul?"* www.bahaiteachings. org. Reprinted with Permission.

8. Jean-Yves Leloup, *The Gospel of Thomas: The Gnostic Wisdom of Jesus,* Inner Traditions; New edition February 16, 2005.

9. Hugh Leroy Thompson, *My Ego,* 1998.

10. Nadia Colburn, *The Inspiring Power of the Haudenosaunee Thanksgiving Address for 2022.* Accessed 2-26-2023.

11. Hugh Leroy Thompson, *The Seeking God,* Sermon, 1997, source unknown.

12. Kahlil Gibran, *The Prophet.* Alfred P. Knopf, New York City, U.S., 1923.

13. Thich Nhat, Hanh, *Peace is Every Step: The Path of Mindfulness in Everyday.* Random House Publishing Group (March 1, 1992).

14. Sidney Jourard, *The Transparent Self* (New York: Van Nostrand Reinhold, US, 1972).

15. John B. Cobb, Jr., *The Faith That Kills and the Faith That Quickens Life,* in Liberal Christianity at the Crossroads (New York: Bantam Books, 1992).

16. Jon Kabat-Zinn, *Wherever You Go There You Are: Mindfulness Meditation in Everyday Life* (Hachette Books, New York, New York City, 2009).

17. www.merriam-webster.com.

18. Bellow, Saul. *Humboldt's Gift.* Published by The Viking Press, New York. 1975.

19. John Steinbeck, https://libquotes.com/john-steinbeck/quote/lbq5n3d. Accessed 7-18-2021.

20. Zig Ziglar, popular motivational speaker, has been given credit, but he has only one variation. Source is unknown.

21. Leonard Sweet, and Frank Viola, *Jesus Speaks: Learning to Recognize and Respond to the Lord's Voice,* (Nashville, TN: Nelson Publishing). 2016.

22. Stephen Hawking, *If you feel you are in a black hole, don't give up. There's a way out,"* www.theguardian.com, 26 Aug 2015.

23. James Manktelow, *Mind Tools,* (Emerald Group Publishing, Leeds, England). 1995.

24. Michelle Obama, *Becoming* (New York: Penguin Random House, 2018).

25. Rumi, www.rumi.org.uk/quotes/. Accessed 10-03-18.

26. *Kintsugi: The Centuries-Old Art of Repairing Broken Pottery with Gold. My Modern Met.* April 25, 2017. Archived from the original on October 10, 2018. Wikipedia.

27. *Oprah Talks to Maya Angelou,* O Magazine, December 2000.

28. www.dodreads.com/cadences/marine-corps-cadences/. Accessed 4-6-2019.

29. www.quotes.net/movies/leap_of_faith_655031.

30. Allan Moyle, director, *Man in the Mirror: The Michael Jackson Story.* Original Release (Paramount Pictures, USA, August 6, 2004).

31. Thomas Jay Oord, *God Can't: How to Believe in God and Love After Tragedy, Abuse, and other Evils,* (SacraSage Press, Grasmere, ID, 2019). 53.

32. Twelve Steps and Twelve Traditions, AA World Services New York, (February 10, 2002).

33. ibid, Step Nine, 83-87.

34. Mark Cartwright, "Narcissus." *World History Encyclopedia*. Last modified March 05, 2023. https://www.worldhistory.org/Narcissus/.

35. C. S. Lewis, *The Great Divorce* (MacMillan Publishing Co., Inc., 1976). 121–22.

36. Albert Schweitzer, *Civilization and Ethics* (UK: Unwin Books). 1961

37. Henri J. M. Nouwen, *Inner Voice of Love: A Journey Through Anguish to Freedom* (New York: Doubleday, 1998). 5.

38. E.F. Beall, "The Contents of Hesiod's Pandora Jar: *Erga* 94–98,» Hermes 117 (1989). 27–30.

39. Thomas Moore, *Soul Mates: Honoring the Mysteries of Love and Relationship* (New York: HarperCollins Publishers, 1994). 95.

40. Kahlil, Gibran, *The Prophet* (Alfred P. Knopf, 1923).

41. Thomas Jay, Oord, *Pluriform Love: An Open and Relational Theology of Well Being,* (SacraSage Press, Grasmere, ID 2022). 160–162.

42. Helen Keller, and Anne Sullivan, *The Story of My Life* (New York: Doubleday, Page & Co., 1903).

43. Claudia Stone, Weissberg, *A 'Bridge' Too Far? Not When It's as Good as Wilder's Novel,* The Pulitzer Prizes, www.pulitzer.org/article/bridge-too-far-not-when-its-good-wilders-novel. Accessed 2/26/2020.

44. *Truth of the Heart: An Anthology of George Fox* Edited by Rex Ambler paperback: (Publisher: QuakerBooks, U.K. January 4, 2007).

45. Leo, Rosten, *The Joys of Yiddish,* First edition, (publisher McGraw-Hill, New York, 1968).

46. Deborah, "Exploring Mother Teresa's Life, from Sister to Saint," *Inside the Vatican Magazine*, March 15, 2016.

47. ibid

48. Leo Buscaglia, www.twosouthernsweeties.com/most-caring-child/. Accessed 7/20/2022.

49. Heart Touching Story, www.wisdomquotesandstories.com/heart-touching-inspirational-story/. Accessed 10/12/21.

50. C. S. Lewis, *Miracles* (London & Glasgow: Collins/Fontana, 1947, 1960).

51. C. S. Lewis, *The Abolition of Man* (New York: Macmillan, 1947). 1s 4, 30.

52. *Canticle of the Creatures,* in *Francis of Assisi: Early Documents*, vol. 1, (New York-London-Manila, 199). 113-114.

53. Oord, *Pluriform Love*, 131.

54. Oord, *God Can't*, 88.

55. Dalai Lama, *The Art of Happiness, 10th Anniversary Edition: A Handbook for Living* (Riverhead Books, 2019).

56. Hugh Leroy Thompson, *Parable*, © 2003.

57. D. W., Winnicott, *The Child, the Family, and the Outside World* (Middlesex 1973). 228.

58. Stanley Hauerwas, *Unleashing the Scriptures: Freeing the Bible from Captivity to America* (Abingdon Press, 1993), 94.

59. Ray Charles and David Ritz, *Brother Ray: Ray Charles' Own Story* (New York: Da Capo Press, 2004), 90–92.

60. Mark. Berman, *'I forgive you.' Relatives of Charleston church shooting victims address Dylann Roof,* (Washington Post, June 19, 2015).

61. Martin Luther King Jr., *The Other America*, https://www.rev.com/ blog/ transcripts. 1997.

62. Nelson Mandela, *Long Walk to Freedom* (Back Bay Books, 1995).

63. Edith Ohaja, www.edithohaja.com/its-a-new-day-poem/ (reprinted with permission).

64. Will Campbell, *Vocation as Grace,* in *Callings!* edited by James Y. Holloway. (New York: Paulist, 1974), 279-80.

65. https://www.pastorlife.com/common/content.asp. This is one source but not the original. It is considered anonymous.

66. Daniel K. Held, *So What Happens When We Assume?* in *Love Does Not Control: Therapists, Psychologists, and Counselors Explore Uncontrolling Love* (SacraSage Press, 2023), 269.

67. ibid, Held, 272.

68. Oord, *God Can't*, 53.

69. William P. Young, *The Shack: Where Tragedy Meets Eternity* (Windblown Media, 2007).

70. Hugh Leroy Thompson, *A Meditation on Love,* © 2001.

Bibliography

Bellow, Saul. *Humboldt's Gift.* Published by The Viking Press, New York, 1975

Booth, Leo. *When God Becomes a Drug.* Los Angeles: Jeremy P. Tarcher, 1991.

Campbell, Joseph. *The Power of Myth.* Doubleday, 1988.

Campbell, Will. "Vocation as Grace." In *Callings!* edited by James Y. Holloway and Will D. Campbell, 279–80. New York: Paulist, 1974.

Cobb Jr., John B. "The Faith That Kills and the Faith That Quickens Life." In *Liberal Christianity at the Crossroads.* New York: Bantam Books, 1992.

Cousins, Norman. *Anatomy of an Illness.* New York: W.W. Norton & Co., 1979.

Dyer, Wayne. *There's a Spiritual Solution to Every Problem.* New York: HarperCollins Publishers, 2001.

Foster, Richard. *Celebration of Discipline: The Path to Spiritual Growth.* New York: HarperCollins Publishers, 1998.

Fox, George. *Truth of the Heart: An Anthology of George Fox, Revised Edition.* Quaker Books, 2007.

Frankl, Viktor. *Man's Search for Meaning.* Pocketbooks, New York, 1939, 1983.

French, Lachlen Paul. *The Gospel According to Thomas: Christ's Recorded Sayings of Mastery.* Horizon Publishing, Hammond, Indiana, 2011.

Fromm, Erich. *War Within Man: A Psychological Enquiry into the Roots of Destructiveness.* Pamphlet for US Quakers, 1963.

Gibran, Kahlil. *The Prophet.* Alfred P. Knopf, New York, New York, 1923.

Hanh, Thich Nhat. *Peace is Every Step: The Path of Mindfulness in Everyday Life.* New York: Bantam Books, 1992.

Hauerwas, Stanley. *Unleashing the Scriptures: Freeing the Bible from Captivity to America.* Abingdon Press, Nashville, TN, 1993.

Heider, Fritz. *The Psychology of Interpersonal Relations.* John Wiley & Sons, New Jersey, 1958.

Held, Daniel K. "So What Happens When We Assume?" In *Love Does Not Control: Therapists, Psychologists, and Counselors Explore Uncontrolling Love,* 269. SacraSage Press, Grasmere, Idaho 2023.

Hesse, Herman. *Siddhartha.* 1922, Mint Edition, Dover Publications, New York, 2020.

Isenhart, Myra Warren, and Michael Spangle. *Forgiving Others, Forgiving Ourselves: Understanding and Healing Our Emotional Wounds.* Skylight Paths Publishing, West California, 2015.

Jourard, Sidney. *The Transparent Self.* New York: Van Nostrand Reinhold, US, 1972.

Kabat-Zinn, Jon. *Wherever You Go There You Are: Mindfulness Meditation in Everyday Life.* Hachette Books, New York City, New York, 2009.

Keen, Sam. *Hymns to an Unknown God: Awakening the Spirit in Everyday Life.* New York: Bantam Books, 1994.

Keller, Helen, and Anne Sullivan. *The Story of My Life.* New York, Doubleday, Page & Co., 1903.

Lewis, C. S. *The Abolition of Man.* New York: Macmillan, 1947.

Lewis, C. S. *Miracles.* London & Glasgow: Collins/Fontana, 1947, revised 1960.

Leyden, Lori. *The Stress Management Handbook: Strategies for Health and Inner Peace.* Santa Barbara, CA: Create Global Health Press, 2013.

Lama, Dalai. *The Art of Happiness, 10th Anniversary Edition: A Handbook for Living.* Riverhead Books, 2019.

Mandela, Nelson. *Long Walk to Freedom.* Back Bay Books, 1995.

Manktelow, James. *Mind Tools.* Emeral Group Publishing, Leeds, England, 1995.

Moore, Thomas. *Care of the Soul.* New York: HarperCollins Publishers, 1992.

Moore, Thomas. *Soul Mates: Honoring the Mysteries of Love and Relationship.* New York: HarperCollins Publishers, 1994.

Nouwen, Henri J. M. *Inner Voice of Love: A Journey through Anguish to Freedom.* New York: Image Books, Doubleday, 1998.

Obama, Michelle. *Becoming.* New York: Penguin Random House, 2018.

Oord, Thomas Jay. *God Can't: How to Believe in God and Love after Tragedy, Abuse, and Other Evils.* SacraSage Press, Grasmere, ID 2019.

Oord, Thomas Jay, ed. *Love Does Not Control: Therapists, Psychologists, and Counselors Explore Uncontrolling Love.* SacraSage Press Grasmere, ID, 2023.

Oord, Thomas Jay. *Open and Relational Theology: An Introduction to Life-Changing Ideas.* SacraSage Press, Grasmere, ID, 2021.

Oord, Thomas Jay. *Pluriform Love: An Open and Relational Theology of Well-Being.* SacraSage Press, Grasmere, ID, 2022.

Palmer, Parker J. *On the Brink of Everything: Grace, Gravity & Getting Old.* Berrett-Koehler Publishers, Oakland, CA, 2018.

Ray, Charles, and David Ritz. *"Brother Ray: Ray Charles Own Story,"* Da Capo Press, *New York, 2004.*

Riskas, Thomas. *Working Beneath the Surface: Attending to the Soul's Hidden Agenda for Wholeness, Fulfillment, and Deep Spiritual Healing.* Executive Excellence Publishing, San Diego, CA., 1997.

Rolheiser, Ronald. *The Holy Longing: The Search for a Christian Spirituality.* New York: Doubleday, 1999.

Rosten, Leo, *The Joys of Yiddish,* First edition, publisher <u>McGraw-Hill</u>, New York, 1968.

Schweitzer, Albert. *Civilization and Ethics.* London, UK: Unwin Books, 1961.

Steinbeck, John. https://libquotes.com/john-steinbeck/quote/lbq5n3d. Accessed 7-18-2021.

Sweet, Leonard, and Frank Viola. *Jesus Speaks: Learning to Recognize and Respond to the Lord's Voice.* Nashville, TN: Nelson Publishing, 2016.

Tolle, Eckhart. *A New Earth: Awakening to Your Life's Purpose.* New York: Penguin Group, 2006.

Winnicott, D. W., *The Child, the Family, and the Outside World* (Middlesex 1973) p. 228.

Young, William P. *The Shack: Where Tragedy Meets Eternity.* Windblown Media, Newbury Park, CA., 2007.

About the Author

Hugh Leroy Thompson is a retired United Methodist clergyman. During his career, he was an ordained lead pastor of churches in Oklahoma, Georgia, and Arkansas. He was also trained as a first responder to assist with social and personal crises, including the federal building bombing in Oklahoma.

Thompson received certification as a chemical dependency counselor, consultant, trainer, and lecturer. He studied with Dr. Don Blackerby, author and trainer of Neuro Linguistic Programming. Together, they formed a clinical training program. Thompson then became the executive director of a private hospital chemical dependency unit in Oklahoma City. He was appointed vice president of university-church relations at Oklahoma City University, where he counseled and taught several classes.

He is the author of several other books on addiction.

Thompson is the patriarch of a large blended family who have been together for more than four decades. His hobbies include golfing, fishing, and landscaping.